Developing Workplace Skills for Young Adults with Autism Spectrum Disorder

other books in the series

Independence, Social, and Study Strategies for Young Adults with
Autism Spectrum Disorder
The BASICS College Curriculum
Michelle Rigler, Amy Rutherford and Emily Quinn
ISBN 978 1 84905 787 5
eISBN 978 1 78450 060 3

Developing Identity, Strengths, and Self-Perception for Young Adults with
Autism Spectrum Disorder
The BASICS College Curriculum
Michelle Rigler, Amy Rutherford and Emily Quinn
ISBN 978 1 84905 797 4
eISBN 978 1 78450 095 5

Turning Skills and Strengths into Careers for Young Adults with
Autism Spectrum Disorder
The BASICS College Curriculum
Michelle Rigler, Amy Rutherford and Emily Quinn
ISBN 978 1 84905 798 1
eISBN 978 1 78450 096 2

of related interest

The Complete Guide to Getting a Job for People with Asperger's Syndrome
Find the Right Career and Get Hired
Barbara Bissonnette
ISBN 978 1 84905 921 3
eISBN 978 0 85700 692 9

Unemployed on the Autism Spectrum
How to Cope Productively with the Effects of Unemployment and
Jobhunt with Confidence
Michael John Carley
Foreword by Brenda Smith Myles
ISBN 978 1 84905 729 5
eISBN 978 1 78450 158 7

Asperger's Syndrome Workplace Survival Guide
A Neurotypical's Secrets for Success
Barbara Bissonnette
ISBN 978 1 84905 943 5
eISBN 978 0 85700 807 7

Supporting College and University Students with Invisible Disabilities
A Guide for Faculty and Staff Working with Students with Autism, AD/HD,
Language Processing Disorders, Anxiety, and Mental Illness
Christy Oslund
ISBN 978 1 84905 955 8
eISBN 978 0 85700 785 8

Developing Workplace Skills for **Young Adults** with Autism Spectrum Disorder

The BASICS College Curriculum

MICHELLE RIGLER,
AMY RUTHERFORD,
and EMILY QUINN

Jessica Kingsley *Publishers*
London and Philadelphia

First published in 2016
by Jessica Kingsley Publishers
73 Collier Street
London N1 9BE, UK
and
400 Market Street, Suite 400
Philadelphia, PA 19106, USA

www.jkp.com

Library of Congress Cataloging in Publication Data
Names: Rigler, Michelle, author. | Rutherford, Amy, author. | Quinn, Emily,
    author.
Title: Developing workplace skills for young adults with autism spectrum
    disorder : the BASICS college curriculum / Michelle Rigler, Amy Rutherford
    and Emily Quinn.
Description: London ; Philadelphia : Jessica Kingsley Publishers, 2016. |
    Includes bibliographical references and index.
Identifiers: LCCN 2016000981 | ISBN 9781849057998 (alk. paper)
Subjects: LCSH: People with mental disabilities--Vocational education. |
    Autistic people--Employment. | Autistic people--Education (Higher) |
    College students with disabilities. | Vocational guidance.
Classification: LCC HV3005 .R538 2016 | DDC 371.92/6437--dc23
LC record available at http://lccn.loc.gov/2016000981

British Library Cataloguing in Publication Data
A CIP catalogue record for this book is available from the British Library

ISBN 978 1 84905 799 8
eISBN 978 1 78450 097 9

Printed and bound in the United States

5166

CONTENTS

ACKNOWLEDGEMENTS

As we wrap up this very difficult and arduous process of writing a four-year comprehensive curriculum, as a group we would like to sincerely thank everyone who gave us words of encouragement, picked up the slack at work and home, and wouldn't let us give up when all we wanted to do was quit writing.

As we move to the next steps in our work, we would like to thank all the colleges that have already invited us to help them develop programming on their respective campuses. The goal in this work has always been to develop stronger supports at as many campuses as possible. If our work contributes to more colleges developing programs which will in turn support this incredible group of students, then our work has been beneficial. Now, as we move into the employment sector, the goal can be changed from simply finishing school to becoming gainfully employed. We would like to thank all the employers who have given us a chance to educate them about the dependability and quality of employees with ASD and have given students and young adults with ASD a chance to prove their capacity.

Our passion for working with this population of young adults has prompted us to write this curriculum. We are grateful for the opportunity to write this series and are increasingly grateful to those who contact us to ask questions, give feedback and share experiences.

Go forward and do great things.

INTRODUCTION

The prevalence of people with Autism Spectrum Disorder (ASD) continues to grow exponentially each year. Currently, an estimated 1 in 68 people has a diagnosis on the spectrum (CDC 2014), representing a prevalence growth of approximately 119.4 percent from 2000 to 2010 (CDC 2014). While young adults with ASD continue to enter college, gain support through specialized programs (Rigler, Rutherford and Quinn 2015a), learn about their strengths and develop confidence (Rigler, Rutherford and Quinn 2015b), the time has come for them to shift their goals to focus on their careers.

Despite the potential for young adults with ASD to be incredible assets as employees, barriers in the workplace can often limit their progress. After going through the exhaustive process of learning their interests, skills, talents, and workplace strengths in order to obtain employment, their focus shifts by necessity to maintain the position in their chosen career. Indeed, Meeks, Masterson, and Westlake (2015) suggest that while there is evidence of societal good results from the employment of young adults with ASD, they still have considerable difficulty in their efforts to maintain their work. They will encounter barriers in the workplace that their neurotypical peers will likely not have to consider. These workplace barriers, from engaging in an interview to figuring out "water cooler culture," may prevent otherwise prepared, intelligent, and successful individuals from career progress.

Yet, with all of the barriers to employment present for young professionals with ASD, their unique characteristics and strengths can offset the impact of the barriers. Potential and current employers can use the strengths of their employees with ASD to improve work production or systems, and to increase the value of the work itself. Once the strengths of those with ASD are noted, they can be used in the workspace. For employers, these strengths are definite assets; for employees with ASD, their strengths will be the key to them navigating any barriers.

Our goal with this text was to present common workplace barriers experienced by young professionals with ASD, and then to point out how their strengths can assist them in navigating those barriers. Essentially, we set out to create a guide for young adults to use as they transition into and encounter challenges within the workplace.

Obtaining a job is only the first part of developing as a professional—just as there is a process that leads to employment, there are also systems that lead to the retention of that employment. For young adults with ASD transitioning into their first professional roles, and becoming aware of barriers that are likely to be present at work is essential.

Having strategies for responding to these barriers, those that are presented in this text and those that are individually identified by professionals in each of their specific roles, will make it easier to approach problems as they arise.

In Chapter 1, readers will consider finding their professional niche, through exploring neurodiversity in the workplace, and identifying a workplace that fits one's needs and interests. In Chapter 2, we look at the interview process and how there are workplace barriers even as applicants are evaluated for a position. Then, the impact of disclosing ASD at work is discussed in Chapter 3, emphasizing logistic considerations such as why, when, and how one may disclose, and also how accommodations can counteract the impact of ASD on some work aspects. In Chapter 4, readers will be introduced to the professional structure of the workplace, and consider how professional status influences interactions and expectations in the workplace. Chapter 5 addresses workplace stressors, and guides readers through developing strategies for coping with stress. In Chapters 6 and 7, readers will be challenged by the social nuances of the workplace in terms of collaboration and a "water cooler culture." These chapters focus on helping those with ASD recognize their value as team members, both in the sense that to be productive, work demands socializing at times, and in the sense that socializing for the sake of socializing and building relationships is a very influential aspect of maintaining career progress. Finally, in Chapter 8, readers will be able to assess their preparedness to engage in professional development and the potential to shift positions as needed.

As these barriers are introduced in the chapters, lessons are included to provide practical strategies for navigating the barriers. While not every individual with ASD will be challenged by the same elements outlined in this text, those who do will be prompted to realize their strengths in the workplace even as they address these barriers.

The impact of ASD is highly individualized, so throughout this text, various methods are used to convey the important messages. As with any curriculum, we can offer tools, but it is essentially up to the reader to choose to use them properly. Our primary method of reinforcing these concepts for the purposes of this text is to remind students that in any situation, and in any endeavor, it is always important to remember the BASICS—Behavior, Aptitude, Self-care, Interaction, Community, and Self-monitoring.

Each chapter concludes with the BASICS chart, providing a visual representation of the subject matter that is to be reflected on. There is also an opportunity for readers to carry out their own, confidential self-evaluation in the blank chart that follows. After this self-evaluation, readers should be able to develop a set of short-term goals based on the areas of improvement identified in the chart, ideally, areas of strength and areas for potential growth for each section of the curriculum. As young professionals move through the curriculum, this process will help them become better self-reflective, self-monitoring adults. (For an example of how to implement the BASICS chart, see *Appendix A.*)

This text is intended to assist readers through the transition of becoming a strengths-based self-advocate. Professionals who work with people with ASD can also use the information presented here to enable discussions in a classroom setting, group setting, or individual meetings. *Appendix B* provides discussion points and questions that can be used by professionals as they see fit. The information is intended to be a starting point to be used with additional discussion, assignments, videos, etc., to best convey the information to specific student groups. Students using the text can take advantage of the reflection questions and worksheets included throughout the text, to ensure a solid understanding of the topics presented. Students often benefit from consistent practice and consideration regarding new material, and so we have designed this text to reflect this notion. In addition, the information can be used as young people with ASD work through the transition of becoming self-advocates, which can be done independently or with support.

We encourage readers to be creative with the material, and to tailor it to individual needs. While it is written to provide knowledge and information about the positive qualities and strengths of individuals with ASD, there is no limit to the ways in which it can be used within a specific context, and this was our intention.

It is the result of research, and was built on significant feedback from those college students with ASD who did not see their own strengths until after engaging in this work. Because these students are the true experts of ASD, they have given us the purpose and passion to help others with ASD to see their own true potential in this world full of neurodiversity. We hope to provide our shared vision of opportunity and knowledge with individuals with ASD and with those professionals who work with them during this exciting transition.

All worksheets marked with the ⊕ symbol are available for download from the JKP website at www.jkp.com/catalogue/book/9781849057998.

Table I.1 Back to BASICS Template

B	**Behavior** 1 2 3	Comments
A	**Academics** 1 2 3	Comments
S	**Self-care** 1 2 3	Comments
I	**Interaction** 1 2 3	Comments
C	**Community** 1 2 3	Comments
S	**Self-monitoring** 1 2 3	Comments

GOALS

Personal:

Aptitude:

Social:

Chapter 1

FINDING YOUR PROFESSIONAL NICHE

INTRODUCTION

The goal for individuals with ASD used to be to "just get through"—get through middle school without too much bullying, get through high school without incident, get through the week without a meltdown—but that goal is no longer enough. The time has come for the goal to now be to obtain gainful employment in a career field that fits each individual. Young adults with ASD have tremendous skills sets that can be a helpful asset for any company, if the fit is good and if the right supports are in place. Unfortunately, the current unemployment rate for individuals with ASD is an astounding 85 percent (Griswold 2014). When considering the number of individuals employed below their skill level being paid less than they deserve, the combined unemployment/underemployment rate is closer to 90 percent (Wilkie 2013). This alarming rate is not necessarily due to lack of motivation or skills, but more likely attributed to the difficulty with those with ASD finding the right fit.

Companies are now beginning to recognize the strengths associated with ASD, and are recruiting people with ASD to fill specific positions. Some companies, such as the Danish company Specialisterne, are recruiting, training, and coaching individuals with ASD with the specific purpose of improving this unemployment rate. Other companies, such as the mortgage company Freddie Mac, are developing full-time paid internships specifically designed for college students with ASD. And finally, major companies, such as the software companies SAP and Microsoft, are developing work initiatives to specifically hire those with ASD in full-time jobs with the goal of increasing the diversity of their workforce. These companies are not filling these positions with people with ASD as charity or a social responsibility, but because they recognize and value the unique skills this population possesses (Erbentraut 2015).

As more information emerges about ASD and the varying ways individuals process information, it is likely that companies will begin to purposely seek out employees with ASD. These individuals will then have the opportunity to begin the construction of their professional niche based on their identified skills and strengths.

LESSON 1: NEURODIVERSITY IN THE WORKPLACE

The impact of ASD is widely misunderstood and is often viewed as a mystery. However, its traits are not necessarily rare—current prevalence rates tell us that those with ASD make up one of the largest minority groups in the United States (Silberman 2015). While the focus in our recent history has been on finding a cause and a cure for ASD, in reality, the benefits of ASD have been long overlooked.

"Diversity" is a concept that is respected and valued as part of our human experience, and cultural diversity allows us to see the strength and beauty within each cultural experience. Recognizing these differences as contributing factors to what weaves our human experience together adds value and richness to the differences so they can be respected. "Biodiversity" allows us to recognize the genetic variations in species, between species, and within various ecosystems. It also recognizes the detailed relationships between the varying species within specific ecosystems, allowing the sustainability of environments. These aspects of diversity keep our society from becoming stagnant, and protect the health and well-being of our culture.

Another aspect of diversity that should be celebrated is neurological diversity, the specific differences in the ways people take in, process, and express knowledge. Neurodiversity is a biological fact based on evidence (Silberman 2015), and it is what drives the neurodiversity movement. Rather than convincing ourselves that there is one "race," culture, or species that is perfect and that should be the gauge for measuring the validity of all others, we celebrate instead the differences and strengths within each. So, rather than convincing ourselves that there is a "perfect" brain somewhere that operates according to an established norm that all other brains should be compared to (Silberman 2015), we should instead view the differences in the neurological functioning of each brain as the gift of diversity. By changing our perspective, neurological differences that were previously pathologized may be viewed as differences that actually enrich human experience.

Within the workforce, various abilities are favored depending on career expectations. For example, for those working in a large technology company, a detailed, logical, and methodical way of thinking about and processing information would be valued. Conversely, for those working in an elementary school teaching children all day, a creative, collaborative, and social way of thinking would be valued. Neither way of thinking is innately better than the other, but what is expected in the career drives what is expected of the people.

Although this is not true for everybody, people with ASD tend to have a different way of processing information, describing this as detailed, focused and logical, building one detail on another to create an accurate big picture. This way of thinking allows those with ASD to see all the important details that many neurotypical people may miss. And if the task at hand is something cognitively challenging and interesting to those with ASD, they are often able to focus for much longer periods of time than a neurotypical person.

Another descriptor often used to explain the thinking style of a person with ASD is as a creative problem solver. This refers to the linear way of thinking that allows someone to identify a glitch in a process and to find a creative and efficient solution. Many companies could benefit from hiring people who think in these ways. Inventors, researchers, scientists, engineers, and technology gurus intentionally seek out this type of thinker, but this style of thinking may also prove generally beneficial in many other settings.

Unfortunately, this style of thinking may also be misunderstood by others, and could create problems. If supervisors are not aware of the level of details being processed, they may misinterpret any subsequent slowdown in work output as lack of motivation. And if colleagues are not aware of the person's logical and scientific way of thinking, they may misinterpret a lack of social communication as the person being rude and aloof.

So, the first step to avoiding this is to develop a solid understanding of your processing style.

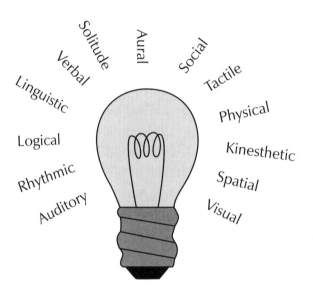

FIGURE 1.1 PROCESSING STYLES

To begin the process of understanding how you, as an individual with ASD thinks, the first step is to examine your preference for taking in information, which can be done by looking at how you sustain attention and retain information. Many individuals with ASD describe being very visual learners and seeing visual images of the information. Temple Grandin (2011) describes this way of thinking as having realistic photos of words stored into categorized folders in her brain that she can flip through, like a slide show. Others would rather have information written down in a very logical and step-by-step way.

Developing an understanding of how you take in information will allow you to begin to explain to others your preferred method for getting information.

Visual (spatial)	You use images to process information
Aural (auditory)	You use what you hear to process information
Verbal (linguistic)	You process things using words, writing and speaking the information
Physical (kinesthetic)	You use your body and senses to process information
Logical	You process information using logic and reason
Social	You learn through social interactions
Tactile	You use physical objects to help process information
Rhythmic	You process using rhythmic patterns
Solitude	You prefer to process information alone

The next step in the process is to develop an understanding of how you process the information once it is received. Typically, those with ASD take longer to process information because they do not have a filter to sort out the important details from additional details (often filtered out by neurotypical people). While this is what allows people with ASD to have significant analysis skills, it does slow down the processing of information. Developing an understanding of why it takes you longer to process information will allow you to explain to others why it may take you longer to respond to a question, and why you need time to develop a suitable response.

The final step in developing a solid understanding of how you think is to identify how you control your knowledge output. Some like to talk through with others about discoveries of solutions, while others prefer to write out detailed logs of steps taken and solutions discovered that can be passed on to others without having to engage in conversation. Both methods share the same information, but the preferred method of sharing the information is very different. Understanding your preferred method and the reason behind it will allow those that work with you to create a set of expectations for how you prefer to communicate professionally.

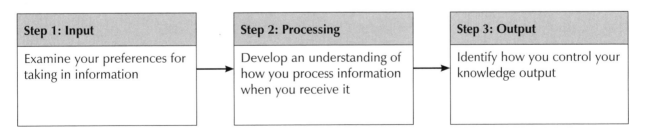

FIGURE 1.2 INPUT, PROCESSING, OUTPUT

While these steps may not help you avoid all pitfalls, they will certainly help you create an air of understanding about yourself in your work environment. By being able to effectively communicate about how you take in, process, and express information to those working with you, you will be able to explain yourself more confidently, and those with whom you work will have a better understanding of the benefits of your thinking style.

Thinking styles may shift according to our work environments and how comfortable we are within each phase of employment, so this process of self-analysis should be revisited to maintain an accurate picture of you as a professional.

Use the following image to begin the discovery process for how you think. Fill in the "input" bubble with how you prefer to receive information, the area around the head with how you filter what is important, and the space outside of the "output" arrow with how you prefer to present information.

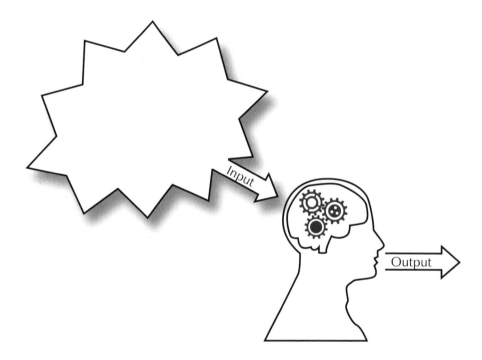

LESSON 2: FINDING A COMPANY THAT WORKS FOR YOU

In the field of theoretical ecology, "niche construction" refers to the activities of an organism that bring about ecologically significant changes to the environment (Scott-Phillips *et al.* 2013). This theory challenges the long-standing theory of natural selection in which an organism must adjust and adapt to its environment for survival. The same can be true for the construction of a professional niche within a chosen career. Historically, workers were expected to adjust to the developed work environment and to adapt themselves in order to survive professionally. This notion is quickly being replaced with more flexible, collaborative work environments meant to acknowledge the differences in the ways people interact with colleagues and management.

The German software company SAP has adjusted its entire interview process to be more problem solving-based, rather than the traditional across the table, face-to-face interviews. This allows people to think creatively, to solve a problem actively while avoiding unnecessary eye contact and scripted interview questions that everyone answers in a similar way. Google has shifted to a more open and innovative workspace by moving it to one floor, reducing the psychological barriers of interacting with colleagues and management. Google has also invited workers to create their own workspace through the use of movable office furniture resembling Tinkertoys. Some workers have designed stand-up workstations while others have created more enclosed workstations (Stewart 2013). Even within some government departments, former isolated beige cubicles are being replaced by collaborative pods of desks, to encourage communication and innovation. While this move is helpful in encouraging teamwork, it may not, however, be the most effective approach for all. Some, for example, may prefer the isolated nature of a small office in which they can more easily control environmental factors around them.

To be able to effectively link your strengths as an individual with ASD to the company's aims, you must first be able to identify your own specific needs for your work environment. And rather than you yourself expecting to have to adjust to the work environment, you are in a position to be able to investigate many different companies, to find the environment that works best for you.

Imagine your perfect work environment that you would enjoy going to every day. The "goodness of fit" is vital—not only must you as a worker have the strengths and skills necessary to complete the expected professional tasks, but your work environment must also be a good fit to sustain you as an individual with ASD.

Although it is likely that no company will be the "perfect fit," having an idea of your needs ahead of time should allow you to search for the right environment for you, instead of you forcing yourself into an environment in which you have to adjust.

Use your image of your perfect work environment to fill in the following professional compatibility checklist, which describes your individual needs. Look into several companies using this checklist, via the companies' websites, and visits, to determine the most compatible environment for you. (It is likely that you will not be able to address all of these components to determine compatibility before interview, as some relate specifically to the individual role within the company.)

As you go through the job search process, add to this checklist with any additional information to help you make a final decision regarding compatibility. Rank compatibility from 0–2, with 0 being not compatible with your needs, 1 being partially compatible, and 2 being the most compatible.

PROFESSIONAL COMPATIBILITY CHECKLIST

Company name:

_____

0 Not compatible, 1 Partially compatible, 2 Most compatible

Compatible	Need	Description
	Is there a commitment to neurodiversity/diversity?	
	What are the expected work hours?	
	What will your workspace look like?	
	How much independent work will you do?	
	How much collaborative work will you do?	
	What will the communication/feedback be like with your supervisor?	
	What support is available to workers?	
	What environmental factors will you need to control?	
	What is the commute time to this company?	
	Other information/questions:	

After investigating several companies for compatibility, compare those scores and determine your top list of companies. This can serve as a starting point for your job search. Take note of the distinct differences between each company, and use this information as a way to prepare for a potential interview. Make notes on the lines below to help guide you in your search.

_____

_____

_____

_____

_____

_____

_____

_____

_____

LESSON 3: CREATING YOUR OPTIMAL WORK ENVIRONMENT

To be a responsible and effective employee, individuals with ASD must take control of creating their optimal working environment. Rather than expecting your specific skills and strengths to mask your individual needs, identifying your needs, advocating for yourself, and creating your work environment to fit your specific needs is the most effective way of creating a positive work culture. Adults spend the most time each day at work, so it should be a rewarding and comfortable place to spend this time.

Use the following scenarios regarding creating an effective or ineffective work environment to begin the discussion of constructing your optimal working environment. Evaluate how the people in the scenarios managed their own work environment, and use their experiences to guide your analysis of your own professional needs.

TOM'S STORY

Tom grew up dreaming about becoming a firefighter. Even as a young child he was fascinated by fire safety and always enjoyed any opportunity to help others. That passion followed him into his young adulthood. Even though he knew his dream job would not require a college degree, it was strongly encouraged. Tom decided he would attend the community college in his area and major in fire science. He acknowledged that not only would he have to do well in school, but he would also need to pursue additional training opportunities and, of course, volunteer in his community, so that he could be considered for a position that might open up once he graduated. Although he enjoyed the journey, Tom did face some challenges along the way.

Tom has some significant sensory sensitivities. He never really adjusted to the loud sirens, felt claustrophobic in his mask during drills, and struggled to adjust to shift changes, but he would let nothing stand in his way of following his dreams. After going through all the training and making connections in his community, his hard work paid off. He was offered a position at Station 7 as a fire lieutenant.

Six months went by, and although he enjoyed the job, it didn't seem like a good fit for him. Firefighters work 48 hours on, 72 hours off, with an extra day off thrown in once a month. Tom had a hard time adjusting to the lack of routine, which had been important to him in the past. One of his professional mentors, someone he had always looked up to, had a conversation with Tom late one afternoon. His mentor had noticed a change in Tom. His attitude about work and at work had shifted. Tom still had passion, but he was struggling. His mentor pointed out that Tom was one of the best on the squad at calming people down in crisis situations, he was really good at building rapport in the community, and had a talent for figuring out where and how fires started. He was always very attentive during training, and paid close attention to minor details that others often missed. He liked interacting with individuals in the community, but seemed to get overwhelmed talking in large groups. Tom thought about the feedback, and decided it might be time to consider a career change.

Tom did some investigating and found a position that allowed him to still have some duties as a firefighter, but that also allowed him the opportunity to use his skills set more appropriately. Tom was a good problem solver, attentive to details, very knowledgeable about the science of fire, and loved finding answers for people. He eventually pursued the necessary training and became a fire inspector. Tom has now been employed with the fire department for 20 plus years, and every day he goes to work with a smile on his face. He doesn't have to worry about shift changes because he works a 9 to 5 job and is on call, which means that he only gets calls after hours when there is a crisis. He is able to stay connected with the relationships he built early on in his career because he collaborates with the others at Station 7 on a weekly basis.

What personal needs should Tom have considered before taking the position as a firefighter?

_____

_____

_____

_____

What strengths should Tom have highlighted in his career search?

_____

_____

_____

_____

How was Tom able to combine his passion and strengths, as well as protect his needs?

_____

_____

_____

_____

ROY'S STORY

Roy loves researching things that are interesting to him. Although he was unsure of what he wanted to major in, he always knew he wanted to seek a college degree. During his years as an undergraduate he developed a fascination with turning his passion for research into a career. He began asking questions, and eventually reached out to the librarian at his university. As he began to learn the logistics behind being a librarian, he also learned that there was a business element. Because of his direct communication style and his ability to negotiate, he knew that he would excel as a librarian. Roy quickly learned that not only did he have a passion for this work, but also, he was really good at it.

He realized that he would need to pursue a master's degree, so he started researching suitable programs.

Roy eventually graduated with a master's degree in Library and Information Science. His first job out of college really took a toll on him, though. At times he found himself working 40 plus hours a week and would go home every night, completely exhausted. He spent a lot of time trying to meet the demands of his administration. He felt he had to answer emails on the weekend, and never felt that he caught up. He tried his best to connect with his co-workers, but rarely invested in building relationships with them due to his social exhaustion. He had a hard time interpreting non-verbal social cues and seeing the value in small talk conversations. Eventually Roy reached out to his supervisor and expressed how he was feeling and his concerns.

After several conversations with his supervisor, Roy realized that the position he was in was not a good fit. He left his position and immediately started seeking new job opportunities. He found an opening at another library, applied, and was granted an interview. During his interview, Roy communicated the many strengths that made him a competent librarian. When asked about the reason why he had left his last position, he was open about the challenges he had faced. He disclosed his ASD diagnosis, and how he has learned to adapt to various situations as a professional. Roy requested accommodations such as working a four-day week to give him an extra day to decompress, direct feedback to give him the opportunity to improve, and detailed communication regarding what was expected of him. Roy was offered the position and he accepted. After six months Roy could tell a difference from his last position, and was happy that he had chosen to disclose and to advocate for his needs. His supervisor entrusted him with more responsibility, and Roy felt relaxed and efficient in his role. His decompression time allowed him to come to work in a positive mood, and he even began to socialize more with his co-workers.

What potentially impacted the success of Roy in his first job?

_____

_____

_____

_____

What strengths did Roy have that made him a good candidate for this career as a librarian?

_____

_____

_____

_____

What was the difference between the approaches Roy took in his first job versus his second job that made it a more successful experience?

_____

_____

_____

_____

JAIME'S STORY

Jaime was recently hired at a technology firm. The only workspace available was a cubicle in the back corner of the office. The supervisor was concerned that Jaime would feel isolated as a new employee, and promised to find her another space when it became available. Jaime moved into her new cubicle at the back of the office, and found that she enjoyed her new work setting very much. Because the cubicle was located in a secluded area, she was less distracted and able to get more work done. When another office space became available, Jaime's supervisor moved her in order to make her feel more connected to her co-workers. As time went by, Jaime's work performance declined. She started coming in earlier in the morning and leaving later to get work done, and left feeling exhausted. Social interaction with her co-workers was difficult for her, and although she was collaborating more with her co-workers, she was not as satisfied, and often felt frustrated. Jaime approached her boss and asked to be moved back to the cubicle at the back of the office. She discussed her distractibility, frustration, and exhaustion. Jaime's supervisor agreed to relocate her under the condition that they work out a plan to make time for team collaboration. They decided that she would attend weekly team meetings and partner on projects when the opportunity became available, but that she would still be able to spend the majority of her time working alone. The plan was implemented, and Jaime found she was more productive and connecting well with her co-workers.

What was the ideal work environment for Jaime?

_____

_____

_____

_____

What steps did Jaime take to find her ideal work environment?

_____

_____

_____

_____

What are some other ways that Jaime could engage with co-workers to make herself feel like part of the team?

_____

_____

_____

_____

What are some ways you can communicate to your supervisor about your work environment needs?

_____

_____

_____

_____

LESSON 4: PROFESSIONAL TOOL FOR NICHE DEVELOPMENT IN A CAREER

Although beginning a career can be overwhelming and a little scary, if you have a set of tools that have been developed and vetted by a mentor, you may be able to better navigate the transition into a career that is both fulfilling and a good fit. This chapter has focused on analyzing work environments and creating a professional niche that may lend itself to a higher chance of professional success for those with ASD. While many companies purposely seek professionals with ASD to fulfill roles developed to highlight the inherent strengths, these options may not always be available in your community. By focusing time and energy early on in your career path on niche development, you may be better prepared to discuss your passions, strengths, and talents, which could allow for a more successful entrance into the world of work.

This example of professional niche development takes into account talents, skills, interests, and previous work experience to create a solid career choice for those with ASD. It is vital to maintain motivation within a career for a person with ASD, so using this tool should encourage you to responsibly combine all three areas to form a balanced professional life.

You will notice that the center of this diagram is labeled "career" which represents a long-term commitment to professional development. The smaller area labeled "passion" represents maintaining our passion to protect and grow our career trajectory. These growth activities contribute to the sustaining of a career. Finally, you will notice that a proper combination of the various aspects of this diagram allows for the creation of "passion." While the daily work duties of any job may not create or sustain your passion, maintaining focus on this balance can also help you sustain your passion.

Use the following as an example for developing your professional niche. After determining how to fill in each section, it can be used as the first tool in your career development toolbox.

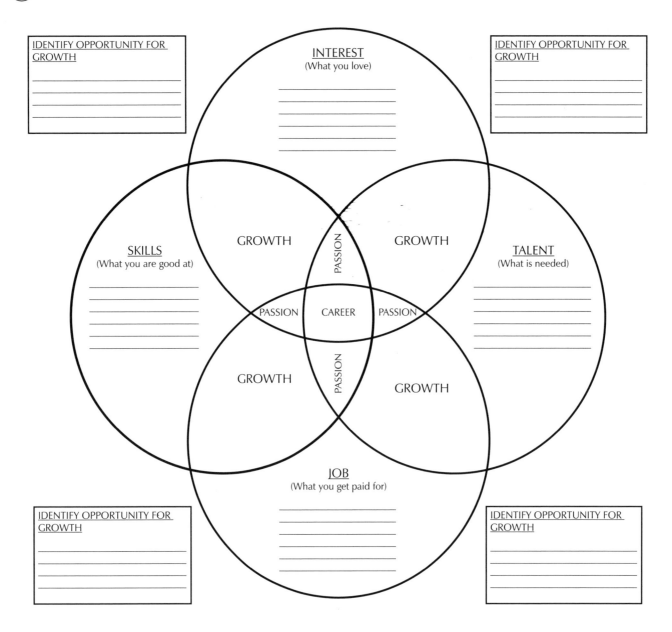

IDENTIFY OPPORTUNITY FOR GROWTH

IDENTIFY OPPORTUNITY FOR GROWTH

INTEREST
(What you love)

SKILLS
(What you are good at)

TALENT
(What is needed)

GROWTH

GROWTH

PASSION

PASSION   CAREER   PASSION

GROWTH

PASSION

GROWTH

JOB
(What you get paid for)

IDENTIFY OPPORTUNITY FOR GROWTH

IDENTIFY OPPORTUNITY FOR GROWTH

The analysis of your personal talents, skills, and interests will help you ensure that these important components of motivation are maintained. By also focusing on your previous work experience, you can present yourself as a qualified candidate, who is able to bring something beneficial to the company.

BACK TO BASICS

B 1 2 3	**Behavior**	Can you identify how you process information? Can you identify your thinking style? Are you actively seeking to identify your professional niche? Are you presenting yourself as a professional?
A 1 2 3	**Academics**	Are you aware of how you take in information? Are you implementing your skills set appropriately? Do you see yourself as capable and competent to perform your duties?
S 1 2 3	**Self-care**	Are you getting enough sleep? Are you eating healthily? Are you maintaining age-appropriate hygiene? Are you planning for your self-care activities? Do you feel comfortable in your professional role?
I 1 2 3	**Interaction**	Are you accepting critical feedback? Are you contributing in a positive way to your workplace culture? Are you collaborating with others to produce a more desirable outcome?
C 1 2 3	**Community**	Do you value your co-workers' roles? Do you feel connected? Are you advocating for the various forms of diversity in your workplace? Are you effectively communicating your work style to your co-workers?
S 1 2 3	**Self-monitoring**	Are you striving to maintain your ideal work environment? Are you actively using your skills set on the job? Are you thinking of your passion and special interests as you develop your professional niche?

GOALS

Personal:

Aptitude:

Social:

BACK TO BASICS: RATE YOURSELF

B	**Behavior** 1 2 3	Comments
A	**Academics** 1 2 3	Comments
S	**Self-care** 1 2 3	Comments
I	**Interaction** 1 2 3	Comments
C	**Community** 1 2 3	Comments
S	**Self-monitoring** 1 2 3	Comments

GOALS

Personal:

Aptitude:

Social:

Chapter 2

THE INTERVIEW

INTRODUCTION

As young professionals look toward the job search to find their first opportunity to begin their career, much attention is focused on building a stellar resume. If you haven't already created your professional resume, see the example template of a complete resume in *Appendix C*. The resume should include educational highlights, internships, volunteer experience, and work experience. Although on paper many people will appear highly qualified for each job opening, and a solid resume can be the ticket to an interview, it is the interview that will get a person a firm job offer.

Once you have been vetted and deemed qualified for the job, you will be called in for the first round of interviews. This is the time when the potential employer is looking for a connection with the interviewee. If there is a potential for a professional relationship or there is some type of connection, you will have a better opportunity for getting an offer. Conversely, if you struggle with non-verbal communication, lack eye contact, and do not connect personally with the interviewer, the impact could be negative.

Neurotypical jobseekers often depend on and place value on interpersonal connections during the interview process, which may mean recognizing pictures on the interviewer's desk, shared interests in a sports team or hobby, engaging in small talk about where the person earned a degree, or simply being polite and engaging in initial conversation.

Individuals with ASD tend to focus on communicating about academic success and specific skills, as these are areas identified as success indicators. The interview experience can be difficult for people with ASD because the focus is on the individual, and a connection may not be established. Without a personal connection, the job may be offered to another applicant, who may or may not be more qualified. So, during the interview, employers are not only looking for the most qualified person, but also for goodness of fit, and will seek out the person who purposely makes a connection, and who will be a good member of the existing team.

This chapter provides some useful information on preparing for interview, how to make a connection with the interviewer, and giving yourself the best chance of getting a job offer.

LESSON 1: PREPARATION FOR INTERVIEW

The first step in preparing for an interview to be successful is to do research about the company on their website. The story of everything the company respects and is committed to will be told through their website. This is the time to identify what is important to the company, and to align the discussion about your strengths with those identified points of interest. As you continue your preparation for the interview process, find out as much as possible about the job for which you are applying.

While there are many questions that are asked fairly consistently in interviews, your responses to these questions must be adjusted for each particular job. Be aware of how your responses represent you and your qualifications, as well as how they match the expectations of the position. Although the preparation work expected prior to an interview is quite significant, it could have a positive impact on the interview experience. The more committed you are to this prep work, the more committed you will be in the interview, and this will be evident to a potential employer (Rigler *et al.* 2015c).

Complete the following interview information card for each interview. By putting the important information in writing, you can remove any stress attached with remembering the details of the interview, thus allowing you to focus solely on interview preparation and on making connections.

 INTERVIEW INFORMATION CARD

Job applied for:

_____

Company name:

_____

What is the benefit of partnering with this person on a team?

_____

Date of interview:

_____

Time:

_____

Interviewer name(s):

_____

Location:

_____

Directions:

_____

Contact number or email:

_____

Special instructions:

_____

Preparing in this way for an interview with each specific company may help avoid any potential roadblocks in the interview process. By researching the company, the expectations, and leadership of the company, you should be able to identify some areas of common interest, and can prepare and rehearse some talking points prior to entering the interview. Through such solid preparation, you should be more confident in the discussion points, which will allow for a more engaging interview process. By approaching the interview with enthusiasm, you will demonstrate that you are invested and want to work with the company. It is equally important, however, to demonstrate authentic enthusiasm. It is easy to tell when people are faking it, and this could impact the interview process negatively. Through your research of the company in advance, you may find some interesting facts that will generate authentic enthusiasm on your part.

Practice interviews as often as possible. Video yourself practicing your interview skills, and critique yourself according to the following job interview evaluation form. Do the same thing with someone you trust who will give you valid and honest feedback using the same form, and compare the two results. Adjust your responses accordingly, and practice again so that when you take part in an actual interview, it should be a more comfortable experience. Use the following job interview evaluation form to monitor your progress in preparation.

 ## JOB INTERVIEW EVALUATION FORM

Interviewee name:

_____

Date:

_____

Position:

_____

First impression Comments:	Poor	Fair	Average	Good	Excellent
APPEARANCE	Poor	Fair	Average	Good	Excellent
Dress Comments:	Poor	Fair	Average	Good	Excellent
Grooming Comments:	Poor	Fair	Average	Good	Excellent
Body language Comments:	Poor	Fair	Average	Good	Excellent
Eye contact Comments:	Poor	Fair	Average	Good	Excellent
COMMUNICATION	Poor	Fair	Average	Good	Excellent
Voice tone Comments:	Poor	Fair	Average	Good	Excellent
Concise verbal communication Comments:	Poor	Fair	Average	Good	Excellent
Non-verbal communication Comments:	Poor	Fair	Average	Good	Excellent
LISTENING	Poor	Fair	Average	Good	Excellent
Answers questions appropriately Comments:	Poor	Fair	Average	Good	Excellent
QUALIFICATIONS	Poor	Fair	Average	Good	Excellent
Discuss education Comments:	Poor	Fair	Average	Good	Excellent
Discuss experience Comments:	Poor	Fair	Average	Good	Excellent
Discuss added skills Comments:	Poor	Fair	Average	Good	Excellent
Overall Concluding comments/feedback:	Poor	Fair	Average	Good	Excellent

LESSON 2: MAKING A CONNECTION

The process of making a connection with interviewers can occur at three distinct but very important times. You can make a personal connection during the introduction phase, the interview process, as well as at the end of the interview. Each of these phases is equally important, so preparing for how a connection can be made can have a positive and lasting effect. Without a good first impression, you may not have the opportunity to be viewed as a valid candidate. During the interview process, if you do not make a connection, you may, perhaps, be seen as aloof and not committed. At the end of the interview, if you do not make a connection, you may easily be forgotten. The number of qualified candidates seeking jobs will more likely be higher than the jobs available at a company, so it is imperative that those with ASD find a way to appropriately stand out and to be remembered.

To begin your interview on a positive note, remember to introduce yourself. This might seem like a simple task, but when you are nervous, the simplest tasks are the ones we forget. So, introduce yourself, shake hands, and look in the direction of the interviewer(s). Use a sincere greeting, such as, "Hello, nice to meet you. My name is Michael, thank you for having me today." Keep in mind that the process of an interview is a tension-causing experience. Not many people go into an interview fully confident, but it is important to present yourself as confident. This means standing tall, shaking hands firmly, and smiling at the interviewer(s). If you can come across as confident in this introductory phase, the interviewer(s) may have more respect for you for the rest of the interview.

You could also make a good first impression by complimenting the office location, architecture of the building, or ease of parking. At this point, however, it is not advisable to compliment any personal attributes of any individual conducting the interview, which may be viewed as insincere and possibly even insulting.

The following are some examples of complimentary statements during the introductory phase of the interview process:

✓**Good**

"Thank you so much for having me today. I have never been in this building, and I just love all the natural light from the windows. It makes for a great working environment."

X **Bad**

"Thank you so much for having me today. I like the color of your hair, it matches your dress perfectly."

✓**Good**

"Thank you for giving me such clear directions to the building. I have never been to this part of town, but your directions made it very easy to find."

X **Bad**

"I see you like the New York Yankees, they are my favorite hockey team too."

While the examples given here are really neither inherently good nor bad, at this phase of the interview process you should not be focused on the physical attributes of a potential employer. This may be seen as arbitrary, disingenuous, or even insulting if the wrong wording is used. The focus of any communication at this point should be on the company or location of the interview, and not on the person conducting the interview.

If you do not know about a sports team or a specific hobby that you can see evidence of in someone's office, don't attempt to compliment the person on this. It is not something you can prepare ahead of time for. It is something that should occur naturally, but if you don't see this connection, don't try to make it happen.

Develop your own introductory statement that could help you connect with a potential interviewer:

_____

_____

_____

If you are being interviewed by a group of people, be sure to introduce yourself and acknowledge each person in the room. You want to establish an understanding that each person in the room is important to the process, and deserves to be equally recognized. Shake hands with each person, smile, and thank them for being there. It is appropriate to recognize some members through non-verbal cues such as a head nod, smile, or a small wave.

During the interview process, you can make a significant and memorable connection with each interviewer. By researching what the company views as important, you can then tie your personal strengths to those important aspects of each company. As a person with ASD, the significant strengths that tend to go along with ASD can be of significant benefit at this time of the interview process. Understanding your particular strengths, and how they could help a company, should make you a truly viable candidate. To find out what each company views as important, look for the company's mission and vision statement on their website.

On Google's website,[1] the following mission statement is highlighted:

> Google's mission is to organize the world's information and make it universally accessible and useful.

Use this information to understand the company's commitment and how your strengths can help meet that commitment.

A good first step in this process is to identify the key words in each mission statement. In the above example, they can be identified as **ORGANIZE**, **ACCESSIBLE**, and **USEFUL**. Once the key words are identified, tie them with your own individual strengths and create statements to share in the interview. A common strength for people

---

1 See www.google.com/about/company

with ASD is the ability to organize and categorize information in a detailed way, so this could be used in a conversation. Refer to the following card for an example of how to expalin your strengths.

This important information can be detailed on a small notecard to be used as a conversation starter during the interview process that focuses on how your individual strengths tie in to the company's commitments. It can resemble a simple card used for follow-up questions but can also serve as a support to help those with ASD make a valid connection with a representative of the company that is tied directly to their mission and vision statements, those statements that define what the company views as important commitments. This is an example of how such a notecard can be used.

Company mission/vision connection card

Company name:
Google, Inc.

Mission statement:
Google's mission is to organize the world's information and make it universally accessible and useful.

Key words:
Organize, universally accessible, useful

Personal strengths:
My fine attention to detail allows me to organize and categorize large amounts of useful information into a system that makes the search process intuitive and accessible.

FIGURE 2.1 EXAMPLE OF A COMPANY MISSION CONNECTION CARD

Investigate several companies and develop a notecard for each. Make a special note of the key words within each mission statement and how they tie in with your strengths.

Company mission/vision connection card

Company name:

Mission statement:

Key words:

Personal strengths:

To highlight some of your strengths as a candidate, you will also have investigated what is important to the company, and you should therefore be able to have an engaging conversation about how you would be a good addition to the team. This preparation work will show that you are invested in the company, and you then can allow for a personal connection to occur naturally during the interview process.

The connection that can occur at the end of the interview may be more difficult, as this will depend on how the interview has gone. Regardless of how successful the interview process may have been, it is important to be respectful at the end. So, first recognize the cue for when the interview has reached its end. The interviewer will typically ask if you have any further questions about the job, which is a clear indication that the interview is coming to an end.

It is always important to ask questions to show that you are interested in the company, but these questions should not be about salary or time off. The questions should be brief enough that they can be answered simply, but with enough substance to show that you are not asking simply them to check off a step in the process.

When you begin to ask questions about the company, the dynamics of the interview process change. Rather than you being interviewed at this point, the company representatives (the interviewer(s)) are being interviewed to establish a goodness of fit. Ideally ask no fewer than two questions at the end of each interview, to establish continued interest and to show confidence in yourself as a viable candidate.

The following are good examples of questions to ask at the end of the interview, to highlight not only goodness of fit, but also your continued interest in finding out more about the company. Be strategic with your questions, and don't ask a question that has already been answered in the interview:

- How does this company honor its employees' diversity?

- Why is the previous person in this position leaving?

- How do you evaluate the success of your employees?

- In which specific aspects of this company are you invested?

- What is your timeline for a decision, and when can I expect to hear from someone?

Once your questions have been answered and you have shown a good effort in establishing your continued interest in the company, listen for another cue that the interview is over. The interviewer may say something to the effect of, "Thank you for coming in to meet with us today, you should be hearing from someone soon." This is a clear indicator that the interview has come to an end, and it is time to excuse yourself from the room. Occasionally someone will walk you out of the room, but if they don't, this is the time to excuse yourself.

It is your final chance to make a personal connection during the interview process. Create a script for how you can confidently conclude any interview. This should be brief, but leave no confusion about your interest in the company. Once developed and practiced, you should be able to use this closing script with any company with which you interview. After some practice you should be comfortable with the words, but this closure is more than just about the words. Stand confidently, shake hands with each person in the room, and speak the script that you have learned directly to them. Make every attempt to look at each person or make some other form of personal connection with someone in the room before you leave.

Here are some examples of potential conclusion scripts:

"Thank you for taking the time to meet with me. I think my strengths and skills would be a great addition to your company. I look forward to hearing from you in the near future."

"Thank you for allowing me to learn more about your company. I think I can bring a great deal to your work, and I share the commitment your company has outlined in your mission statement. I feel like I am a great fit for your company and hope to hear form you about the potential for employment with you."

Create your own closing script:

_____

_____

_____

_____

_____

As stated several times in this chapter, making a connection is key to getting an offer for employment. They may take added effort on your part, but whether the connection is made in the very beginning of the interview, during the interview process, or at the end of the interview, this connection is vital to make you stand out from the other qualified candidates. Without this connection, you could miss out on a great professional opportunity.

LESSON 3: FOLLOW UP

A final way to make a connection with the interviewer(s) is to follow up with a thank you letter or email. In the follow up it is important to cover four main points (Rigler *et al.* 2015c):

- Format and address the letter or email appropriately, and thank all of those involved for taking the time to meet with you.

- Remind them of the position you interviewed for, and the date on which the interview occurred.

- Briefly reference the skills and experience you have as they relate to the job.

- Express your continued interest in the position.

While many interviewers receive follow-up emails from potential candidates for jobs, it may have more of an impact if you send a written thank you card instead of an email. This should serve as the final way to help you stand out from the other candidates. But if you are concerned about your handwriting, you could type up a message and include it in the card.

Read the following examples of actual thank you letters sent to potential employers, and provide some feedback on how they could be made more effective:

EXAMPLE 1: EMAIL THANK YOU

Joe,
Thanks for meeting with me about the job you have open. I really enjoyed talking to you and the other guys in the interview. I think I can be a good part of the team there and look forward to the opportunity to work with y'all.
Thanks again,
Stuart

How could this thank you email have been more effective?

_____

_____

_____

_____

What do you think "Joe" would remember about "Stuart" from this email follow-up?

_____

_____

_____

_____

EXAMPLE 2: THANK YOU CARD AND LETTER

To whom it may concern,

I was in your office for an interview on November 21, 2015, and met with a man named John, a man named Stanley and a woman named Gina about a job as a computer programmer. I think I'm a good candidate, and look forward to hearing from you with an offer.

Sam

How could this thank you letter have been more effective?

_____

_____

_____

_____

What do you think this team of professionals would remember about "Sam" as a result of this thank you letter?

_____

_____

_____

_____

EXAMPLE 3: THANK YOU CARD AND LETTER

Mr. Smith,

I recently met with you to discuss a potential job with your company, and would like to thank you for your time. I enjoyed discussing the potential for a position as a computer programmer, and I think my programming skills and attention to detail could be of great benefit to your team. I am very interested in lasting employment with your company, and hope to hear back from you soon.

If you have any further questions, please feel free to contact me any time.

Thank you,

Cory

How could this thank you letter have been more effective?

_____

_____

_____

_____

_____

What do think "Mr. Smith" will remember about "Cory" as a result of this thank you letter?

_____

_____

_____

_____

_____

Follow-up after an interview can be more than simply sending a thank you to the interviewers. This is a time when you can ask further questions or clarify an answer to a question.

Here are some scenarios for further interview follow-up possibilities.

ALLIE'S STORY

Allie has been searching for a position in higher education. She recently submitted her resume to the Student Success Office at a metropolitan university in her area. A few weeks later she got a phone call asking her to schedule a Skype interview for the following week. Allie was so excited; she did her research and knew the interview would last about an hour and the interviewers would be a group of professionals from different departments on campus. She looked up common interview questions and practiced by writing out her responses.

It was the day of the interview, and although Allie was nervous, she felt really prepared for the interview. Around 1.00pm, which was 30 minutes before her interview, she began to set up her computer and get things ready. During this process she logged on to her professional Skype account that she had created a few months ago, specifically for interviews. As she was checking to make sure everything was working properly, she realized that her sound was working but her microphone was not. She spent some time trying to fix the problem, but could not figure it out. When she realized it was 1.25pm and the interview was supposed to start in 5 minutes, she quickly drafted an email to send to the interviewers to let them know she was having technical difficulties. She did everything she could think of, and even called the IT department at the school she was interviewing at. She drafted another email and sent it requesting the interview be a phone interview. The interview committee agreed, and Allie started her phone interview 15 minutes late, at 1.45pm.

As the interview started, Allie was flustered and apologized for the delay. The interview was suppose to last an hour but only lasted about 20 minutes. In fact, the interviewers only asked five or six questions. At the end of the phone interview the committee said they would be making their decision in the next few weeks. Now all Allie could do was wait for the committee to make their decision.

What are some things Allie could have done differently?

_____

_____

_____

_____

_____

How might you prepare for a Skype interview?

_____

_____

_____

_____

_____

Allie wants to send a follow-up email to the committee. She wants to apologize for the technical issues and to thank them for their time and consideration. What should she say in her email?

_____

_____

_____

_____

_____

What was the impact of Allie emailing updates and ultimately asking for a phone interview?

_____

_____

_____

_____

_____

CALEB'S STORY

A medical group in town is looking for a clinical trial director. Caleb has experience managing medical offices, and has conducted a few clinical trials at one of his previous jobs. In his free time he loves to research new and innovative approaches to medicine and has a broad range of experience in the medical field.

Caleb applies for the position of clinical trial director, and is invited to participate in the first round of interviews. He does his research on the medical group and prepares for the interview to the best of his ability. Finally, the interview day comes, and Caleb feels really good about how things went during his interview.

Afterwards, he sent a follow-up email thanking the search committee for their time and consideration for the position.

A week went by before Caleb got a phone call. They had liked him and wanted to invite him to the second round of interviews. Caleb was less nervous and more excited now. He felt like he really had a chance to get what he thought could be his dream job.

During the second round of interviews the questions got more difficult and the interviewer focused heavily on Caleb's research experience. Caleb did the best he could, but did not feel as confident as he did in the first round. He was unsure whether or not to send another follow-up email or how long he would have to wait to see if they offered him the position. He decided to be patient and wait a few days before doing anything.

A week-and-a-half later, Caleb got an email letting him know that they had offered the position to someone else.

What type of follow-up should Caleb give to his rejection email?

_____

_____

_____

_____

_____

How can Caleb learn from this experience?

_____

_____

_____

_____

_____

What could Caleb have done differently?

_____

_____

_____

_____

_____

What would be the worst response Caleb could have had to the rejection email?

_____

_____

_____

_____

_____

MARY'S STORY

Mary is a 24-year-old senior in college and is preparing for graduation in a few months. She is currently doing an internship at a local insurance company. Like most graduating seniors, Mary knows that her internship site does not have room at the local office to hire her once she has completed her degree, so she started searching for a full-time position at other agencies.

Mary recently applied for a position as a claims clerk at Wells Fargo. After submitting her resume, she started doing research on the position and the company's mission. When she got a call about scheduling an interview, she was so excited and actually felt prepared, since she had already done the research. She went to the interview and left feeling really good about how things had gone.

She sent a short follow-up email thanking the interviewers for their time and expressing her interest in the position. Two weeks later, she got an email from Wells

Fargo inviting her to the second round of interviews. She accepted, and the following week she had her second interview.

A week later she got a phone call offering her the position. The Wells Fargo representative told Mary to check her email and to respond to accept the position.

Mary knows she got the job. What should she say in the email when she accepts the position?

_____

_____

_____

_____

_____

What are some appropriate questions she could ask in the follow-up email?

_____

_____

_____

_____

What if Mary decides to decline the position? What might she say in her follow-up email?

_____

_____

_____

_____

LESSON 4: PROFESSIONAL TOOL FOR SCRIPTING COMMON INTERVIEW RESPONSES

A final step in being prepared for an interview is to prepare a script for some of the most frequently asked interview questions. The majority of interviews include a variation of a common set of questions, each of which serves a purpose (Green 2015). Five of these questions are outlined here, with the "purpose" of the question defined. An adequate understanding of this should help in developing a good answer, while scripting and practice will help you feel more comfortable with the interview process, which should make the interview stage of the job search less stressful, and could also result in more likelihood of a personal connection with potential employers. Two sample responses to the interview questions are offered for each question to be analyzed.

Script your own responses to each of the five questions following analysis of the presented responses, and add this professional tool to your career development toolbox.

 ## INTERVIEW QUESTION SCRIPTS

Q1: Tell us a little about yourself

Purpose

The reason this question is used as an introduction to the interview process is for potential employers to get a glimpse into how candidates view themselves professionally. This is also a time for the interviewers to discover something interesting about the candidate that can help them remember the candidate. The response should be about one minute long with a little personal information and a little professional information, but not too much of either.

Response 1

"I was born in a small town in Oklahoma in 1963 and have three brothers and a sister. My father was a doctor and my mother was a stay-at-home mom. We moved quite often when I was growing up, so I didn't have a lot of close friends. My parents divorced when I was 15 years old so I had to quickly become responsible and help around the house. After I graduated from high school I went on to college and graduate school where I got my Computer Science degree. I have worked on a lot of projects at home, but I haven't had any professional jobs yet. I also have a deep obsession for Star Wars."

Analysis of response 1

_____

_____

_____

_____

_____

Response 2

"I am a Computer Science major from the University of Tennessee, Chattanooga, and I have worked with a couple of my peers to cultivate a website development firm. I really enjoy the process of developing websites that display the strengths and differences of each of the client companies, so they can best highlight and market their work. We have only been paid to develop two websites so far, but we have seven fully developed websites in our portfolio, if you would like to see any of them. I also like older style video games, so I have recently started using my technical skills to develop variations of old style video games. I can also identify bugs in software and create solutions rather easily. I don't really love doing that, but I can do it effectively."

Analysis of response 2

_____

_____

_____

_____

_____

Your response

_____

_____

_____

_____

_____

Q2: What interests you about this job?

Purpose

This question allows the interviewer to understand how much homework about the company and the job the candidate has done, as well as understand what is important to the candidate as a jobseeker. It is very important not to focus on salary, benefits, transportation, or time off during this phase of the interview. This question helps an interviewer understand if the candidate is someone who would be driven and motivated to do the job well rather than just coming to work to earn a paycheck.

Response 1

"I live very close to this office and because I don't drive, it would make the commute to work easy for me. I have also worked for a subsection of this company because my neighbor owns a company that is a subcontractor for you, and he let me work for him over the summer, so I think I know a bit about your company. I also have checked into the salary of this position and it would be just enough."

Analysis of response 1

_____

_____

_____

_____

_____

Response 2

"In preparation for my graduation I have been researching many openings around the state, and this one seems to be the most interesting to me. I am very passionate about the environment, and I would like the opportunity to develop ways to use the river for energy while also protecting the environment. This job seems like a great way to blend the things that interest me the most."

Analysis of response 2

_____

_____

_____

_____

_____

Your response

_____

_____

_____

_____

_____

Q3: What would you do in your first 90 days on the job?

Purpose

This question is meant to analyze the candidate's ability to observe a work culture, create solutions, and to set goals. While interviewers want candidates to suggest potential changes, they do not want them to set unrealistic expectations or to create chaos in the workplace for the sake of change. It is a good idea to discuss getting to know the team and the workplace culture, analyzing where the needs are, and developing a timeline for changes, as they are needed. It is also a good idea to recommend some specific ideas, but nothing too drastic.

Response 1

"The first thing I would do is talk with as many people as I can to get a true picture of what is happening in the company. Then I would think about what could be made more efficient, and develop a timeline for making a change. I would start making those changes as soon as possible, without making anyone uncomfortable. For instance, I would probably begin with a redesign of your company's website. Not that it is bad necessarily, but it looks generic."

Analysis of response 1

_____

_____

_____

_____

_____

Response 2

"I would just go in and get to work on whatever needs to be done. I take direction very well, so I would meet with my supervisor and ask where I can begin my work. I would make it a point to check in with my supervisor as often as possible until I get a strong understanding of my job. I would try to not make any changes initially until my supervisor tells me it is okay to do so."

Analysis of response 2

_____

_____

_____

_____

_____

Your response

_____

_____

_____

_____

_____

Q4: What are some of your weaknesses?

Purpose

This question allows an interviewer to have insight into a candidate's humility. Many candidates try to answer this question by using a cliché response that doesn't give any insight into how they have grown professionally. Candidates with ASD have the opportunity to present their recognized struggles, but also to offer how they have overcome those difficulties in a solution-focused way. Candidates should be honest and humble in their answers to this question, but only focus on their qualities, and not on the impact that others may have on them within the workplace.

Response 1

"I tend to have some difficulties in the workplace when it comes to distractions. I am easily distracted by sounds around me, and these distractions could get me off task very easily, which could be frustrating for my co-workers and supervisors. In the past, I have solved this by using small earplugs that help me shield the sounds I can hear at work. This allows everyone else to do the work the way they need to, and allows me to have the quiet workspace I need to get work done to the best of my ability."

Analysis of response 1

_____

_____

_____

_____

_____

Response 2

"I have had a difficult time in the past when my colleagues don't work as hard as I do. I tend to put in 110 percent effort in my work, and expect everyone else around me to do the same. I like to think of myself as a perfectionist, but when others don't work as hard as I do, I tend to get upset, and that could cause some difficulty in work relationships. I have found that if I just help my colleagues work as hard as I do, it is a better environment."

Analysis of response 2

_____

_____

_____

_____

_____

Your response

_____

_____

_____

_____

_____

Q5: Why should we hire you over the other candidates?

Purpose

The intention of this question is to allow the candidate one last effort to sell themselves to the interviewer. It is not meant to discount any other individual or potential candidate. Candidates should recognize that they do not know anything about the other candidates, so their answer should focus on their own strengths. Candidates with ASD tend to have very specific skills sets, so should identify how these can help the company above and beyond meeting the expected qualifications for the job.

Response 1

"In the job description, you identified that you are seeking someone who can creatively solve problems within the technical side of the company. I am particularly analytical, and can often recognize the details that others may not intuitively recognize. Because I can recognize those details, I can also identify patterns that can allow for the most efficient pathway to problem solving. Many people can solve problems, but a truly analytical and detail-focused person can be an efficient creative problem solver."

Analysis of response 1

_____

_____

_____

_____

_____

Response 2

"I think I would be the most dedicated person to this company because I am truly a committed person. While relationships and social things may distract other people, I tend to focus solely on my job. This means that I would be the most motivated and effective candidate for the job."

Analysis of response 2

_____

_____

_____

_____

_____

Your response

_____

_____

_____

_____

The interview process is very difficult for any jobseeker. By preparing potential scripts for some of the most frequently asked interview questions, those with ASD can focus more on attempting to make a connection with the interviewer(s). Spend time developing the most complete, honest and impressive scripts to these questions, and practice generalizing the information for other possible interview questions. Always remember to word your responses in a positive way.

BACK TO BASICS

B 1 2 3	**Behavior**	Are you spending time preparing for interviews in advance? Do you come across as confident while practicing your interview skills? Do you demonstrate authentic enthusiasm when responding to practice interview questions?
A 1 2 3	**Academics**	Does your skills set match your job search? Are you confidently projecting your skills set? Do you have a plan to recover from a bad first impression?
S 1 2 3	**Self-care**	Are you getting enough sleep? Are you eating healthily? Is your hygiene acceptable for an interview? Are you maintaining a professional image during your interviews?
I 1 2 3	**Interaction**	Is your body language appropriately portraying your interest in the position? Are you using your skills set to engage in conversation? Do you practice making connections with small talk? Have you scripted your introduction to an interviewer?
C 1 2 3	**Community**	Are you actively seeking to make connections with those in your field? Have you identified people who will give you constructive feedback as you prepare for interviews? Have you researched the companies for which you are submitting applications?
S 1 2 3	**Self-monitoring**	Are you practicing your listening skills? Have you assessed what makes you a qualified candidate for the position? Are you aware of your identifiable strengths? Are you aware and able to identify your weaknesses? Do you plan to disclose your ASD?

GOALS

Personal:

Aptitude:

Social:

BACK TO BASICS: RATE YOURSELF

B	Behavior 1 2 3	Comments
A	Academics 1 2 3	Comments
S	Self-care 1 2 3	Comments
I	Interaction 1 2 3	Comments
C	Community 1 2 3	Comments
S	Self-monitoring 1 2 3	Comments

GOALS

Personal:

Aptitude:

Social:

Chapter 3

DISCLOSURE AND SELF-ADVOCACY

INTRODUCTION

When individuals with disabilities consider their options for employment, many make decisions about whether or not they will disclose that they have a disability to their potential employer. For some, especially for those who have disabilities that are not visible such as ASD, making this disclosure decision is difficult because no one can entirely predict how another person might respond. There are many reasons why someone might tell others that they have an ASD, and there are many reasons why someone might choose to not tell others. While there is no right or wrong decision when it comes to disclosure, young adults on the spectrum should take care in considering how to approach disclosure in their professional lives – especially why, how, and when (Rigler *et al.* 2015c). Seeking accommodations, explaining behavior or communication preferences, and otherwise asking for support with challenges related to having ASD begins with the decision to disclose.

Having control of the support you request for ASD at work can certainly be liberating, but the responsibility that comes with this control can also be challenging. As a young adult with ASD in the workplace, just like in college, not asking for help or asking for help too late can have serious consequences. Employers, just like professors, will not know to help you unless they know you need help. Disclosure, telling others that you have ASD, opens the door for you to receive support through legal protections and accommodations, but this act also generally serves your personal interest as an individual with ASD.

One way disclosure can help is that it provides the opportunity for others who might see your disclosure as a relatable and interesting personal experience to welcome your explanation for behaviors or communication style. Considering the legal protections for young adults with ASD and/or other disabilities in the United States, disclosure leads the way to accommodations and discourages discrimination. But keep in mind that disclosure is also largely a social act, and since workplace social nuances can be challenging for individuals with ASD, this element of disclosing ASD should not be overlooked.

LESSON 1: LEGAL PROTECTION AGAINST DISCRIMINATION AND EQUAL ACCESS TO ACCOMMODATIONS

DISCRIMINATION

Legal protection from discrimination and equal access through reasonable accommodations are available to individuals with disabilities in the United States under the Americans with Disabilities Act Amendments Act 2008 and the Rehabilitation Act 1973. If you don't live in the US, take some time to investigate the disability discrimination laws in your country, and compare them with the information in this chapter about the laws in the US.

While it may not be overt, workplace discrimination can be an issue for individuals with ASD. For example, it may be that someone with ASD discloses their disability and makes reasonable accommodation requests, but that these are denied outright, with no explanation, or perhaps they are not even considered at all. In other cases, employers may demonstrate an outright refusal to consider those with ASD as potential employees at a company because of their disability.

These kinds of discrimination can happen before you are hired, during the hiring process, or after you have started a job. Discrimination may occur at an institutional level or more casually, through interactions with co-workers. Regardless of how it happens or who is responsible for it, it is vital that you have a plan in place to deal with it. You need to know not only the protocol for making a discrimination claim, but also who can support you through the process. Supervisors, human resources (HR) department staff members, and same level co-workers are some options to support you at work, while good friends and family members can help you process the personal implications from any such discrimination.

If you have concerns about discrimination or want to ask your employer about company policies regarding how to report or what constitutes discrimination, speak with your supervisor. If you feel uncomfortable speaking to your supervisor, there may also be an HR department associated with your workplace that is another source for you to work through issues of discrimination or accommodation. Lawyers, civil rights advocates, and mentors are other options in the event that you feel that you have experienced discrimination. In the US there are also federal and state government resources such as the Equal Employment Opportunity Commission and the Office for Civil Rights through the Department of Justice that can investigate your claim and advocate for your rights.

ACCOMMODATIONS

Accommodations are set in place in the workplace in order to afford an individual with a disability equal access to their work environment, materials, and tasks. An accommodation addresses an ASD-related barrier, allowing the individual to perform the essential functions of their job.

Even at the interview phase, accommodations may be a relevant request that you may need to make. Some employees seek formal accommodations such as an altered schedule, while others are more informal and not necessarily based on the employers' legal obligation to provide accommodations. These informal accommodations might simply be the use of headphones in a cubical environment, or frequent feedback, and may be allowed for all employees.

Just as college students must disclose that they have a disability to request accommodations through the disability services resource on campus, a professional who wishes to seek accommodations will similarly be expected to disclose a disability to the appropriate people so that accommodation decisions can be made in the workplace.

While pursuing accommodations for ASD is the employee's responsibility, they will work with their supervisors and/or with the HR department, but should also keep in mind that they will need to be able to perform the essential functions of the position with or without accommodation.

For a summary of some of the major differences between the accommodation process in college and in the workplace, see the following figure.

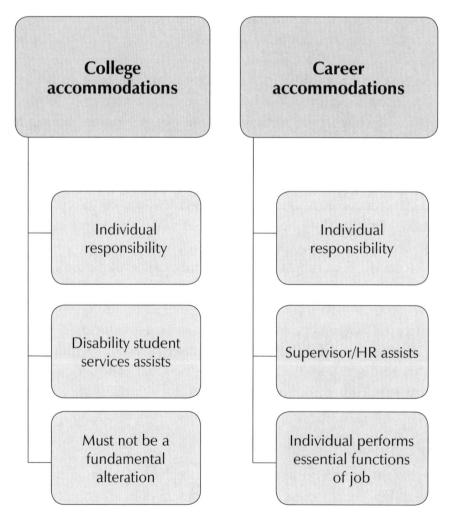

FIGURE 3.1 COMPARING COLLEGE AND WORKPLACE ACCOMMODATIONS

There are many differences in these processes that will be dependent on the culture of the workplace. Reflect on your accommodation experiences in the past, at college, and discuss how you need to structure this process differently in the workplace:

_____

_____

_____

As you contemplate your professional opportunities within different businesses or companies, think about the culture for accommodation that these places provide. It may be that some companies have more resources and funds available to more thoroughly provide accommodations through established departments and personnel, but other businesses may be more adept at handling personal requests without the formality of some of the bigger companies. Accommodations may be formally made with your supervisor and may also involve an HR office representative who is familiar with these processes and employee rights and responsibilities.

During the discussion about accommodations, be prepared to discuss in detail how ASD impacts you at work. You will be asked about the aspects of your position that create barriers for you, so consider what impacts you ahead of this meeting. As you discuss any barriers, your supervisor will work with you to determine some reasonable accommodations to provide equal access for you at the workplace. This conversation will generally be confidential; your accommodations may be known (i.e., a flexible schedule would be obvious to co-workers), but your diagnosis and personal information regarding ASD should remain private, unless you choose to share it with others.

The timeliness of the provision of your accommodations should be reasonable, but be prepared to maintain conversations with your supervisor about your needs as the accommodations process goes forward. You may find that there is an informal way to offset a barrier you are experiencing at work and that you no longer need an accommodation, or that you need an accommodation for an aspect of your position you had not previously experienced.

If you have ideas about accommodations that might be helpful for you to have at work, be prepared to discuss them and explain why the adjustments would allow you the same access as everyone else. Think about the accommodations you had in college, and consider whether there are any similar barriers present in the workplace. If you are just starting a new job, ask questions about the work culture and environment so you can anticipate any barriers ahead of time.

There are certainly many options available for accommodations, and the decisions to implement them will rely on how ASD impacts you individually. Some common workplace accommodations for individuals with ASD at work can also serve as examples of what might be available in the work environment. See the accomodation ideas on the next page and take some time to consider how ASD may impact you at work. Identify what accommodations may be reasonable to provide you with equal access.

Table 3.1 Accommodation ideas for young adults with ASD at work

Common impact of ASD	Possible workplace accommodation
Requires additional "down time" to offset impact of work stress	Flexible work schedule (i.e., three eight-hour days at the office and two eight-hour days at home)
Processes information slowly, completing tasks as individual steps	Provision of reasonable written instructions for multi-step work tasks
Easily distracted	A digital recorder or smart pen to use during meetings
Sensitive to sensory stimuli	Low-stimuli workspace or the use of headphones
Difficulty taking written notes quickly	Use of a laptop or tablet
Lacks understanding of some social rules	Access to a mentor
Other:	
Other:	
Other:	
Other:	

As a young adult with ASD, you may be encountering your first job and making your first decision about disclosing ASD to an employer. You may not have an exact idea of what you need in accommodations or how to request support. It could also be that you do not need to request accommodations. Regardless of your individual circumstances, it is important that you do not approach matters of disclosure or accommodations lightly.

It may be that setting up accommodations "just in case" is worth pursuing as part of your transition plan into a new position. If you choose to set up accommodations and disclose to your co-workers as you enter a new position, it is important that you have a plan and are prepared to discuss your own experience with having ASD (see Lesson 2 that follows).

LESSON 2: ART OF DISCLOSURE

Individuals on the spectrum should be prepared to discuss the impact ASD may have for them in a work environment and while completing work-related tasks, even if there is no immediate need to disclose. A recent study of the career planning experiences for some young adult college students with ASD has led some to contend that understanding one's strengths and limitations is one of the fundamental aspects of disclosure (see Briel and Getzel 2014). Understanding how you work best as an individual with ASD is the first step to being able to showcase your strengths.

Initially, as you consider current employment or future employment possibilities, reflect on the various reasons you may have for disclosing. Once you know *why* you are telling others about ASD, you will be more prepared to tackle two other essential considerations for disclosure: *when* and *how*. Knowing how to adapt to the professional context and when to plan for disclosure in response is an essential part of managing employment for those on the spectrum.

WHY?

People with ASD choose to disclose or not to disclose that they have ASD for a variety of reasons. In the context of your future workplace, disclosure has implications that can impact your work performance, how you approach social interactions, and the way others perceive you. These can certainly influence an employee's decision to discuss ASD with those with whom they work. Those who do decide to tell supervisors, co-workers, and/or HR staff members at the workplace often do so for legal reasons (e.g., in order to obtain accommodations), professional reasons (e.g., to explain behavior or seek clarification), and for the sake of investing in personal relationships. On the other hand, those with ASD may choose not to disclose for a variety of valid reasons as well.

One reason why many employees share ASD with those at their workplace is to set up accommodations. As discussed in Lesson 1, requesting formal accommodations in the workplace is similar to that in college in that the process begins when an employee discloses a disability. In fact, if you need accommodations and do not request them at the beginning of your work experience, you will likely have limited legal protection, such as that offered through the Americans with Disabilities Act Amendments Act 2008 for individuals with disabilities (Hurlbutt and Chalmers 2004). If you are unable to perform the essential functions of your job and fail to uphold your workplace's performance standards due to your decision not to request accommodations, you could lose your job. Thus, disclosure for some individuals with ASD is a formal process through which they request accommodations in order to perform their work, while for others, it may be less formal.

In addition to seeking accommodations, the need to explain behaviors that may be viewed as "odd" by neurotypical co-workers or to seek clarification on social rules also prompts some young adults with ASD to disclose. The desire to share personal information with a friend is another reason. Behaviorally and socially, disclosing ASD may offer some explanation to your co-workers if ASD impacts your understanding of common social rules. Getting to know your co-workers can happen quickly because you spend a great deal of time working with them. You may then get to know some of their quirks, and they may recognize some of yours. If professional friendships develop at work, consider disclosing ASD as you would to any other friend, but be aware of your professional boundaries.

WHEN?

It can be difficult for young adults on the spectrum to determine appropriate times for disclosing ASD in the workplace. This involves interpreting social cues and understanding typical hiring processes. Once you have made a decision to let others know you have ASD, the next decision you need to make is when you want to share the information. Consider who you will tell as you make your decision. Telling co-workers and telling your boss may occur for different reasons and at different times, depending on your reason for disclosing.

Rigler *et al.* (2015b) suggest that young adults with ASD can consider their timing of disclosure around the interview: before, during, or after the interview. If you need accommodations or special considerations for the interview, it is important that you share that with the employer before you arrive for the interview. For example, if you use an app to monitor the volume and tone of your voice, providing a simple explanation ahead of time can prepare both you and those who are interviewing you. In fact, disclosing ahead of time in the case of accommodation needs is a way to demonstrate the self-advocacy skills you have practiced throughout college.

Some young adults choose to disclose that they have ASD during the interview itself. For example, during an interview, a candidate may say:

> "I have ASD and because of that, I am very dependable. Once I set a routine and a schedule, I like to follow that routine. This means that I will rarely be late or miss work. You will be able to depend on me."

Some options for appropriate framing for ASD disclosure during an interview include:

- in your response to the "tell me about yourself" prompt in the interview

- when prompted to describe your strengths and skills

- in your response to questions about your unique qualifications or special interests

- in a question you ask as the interview closes (e.g., "What kinds of support would be available for someone with ASD like myself?" or "I have ASD and prefer structured work environments. How is this company structured during day-to-day work?").

Finally, after you have been hired, you may tell others about ASD for legal, professional, or personal reasons. When you tell others about ASD after having already secured the position, you will likely have gained an understanding of your new workplace's structure, and will have had an opportunity to get to know your professional community. With this knowledge, your disclosure discussion can be directed toward overcoming any barriers you have noticed in your work environment. Also, waiting to disclose until you are hired can allow for a more informal conversation about ASD between co-workers without the added pressure of wondering how employers' awareness of your disability during the hiring process influenced their consideration of you for employment.

HOW?

Once you have made the decision to tell others about ASD after starting work or in advance of or during an interview, consider how you will approach the subject. This will depend on the reason you disclose, to whom, and when. The reasoning for planning ahead for how you will deliver personal information about yourself is largely so that people will not only hear your words, but they will also consider the social context in which you tell them the information. The setting and social dynamic of an important conversation such as disclosure influences how well the message is received. In the case of disclosure, realizing that some of your co-workers may have little or no experience with individuals with ASD is essential. Others may have knowledge of ASD and relate to your disclosure, and some may have questions about it. An important guideline to remember when developing a disclosure plan is that these conversations are best managed privately. Knowing this, you can create disclosure opportunities that provide both you and the person(s) with whom you are speaking with a setting that encourages candid conversation. Prepare for the various outcomes of disclosure conversations by developing scripts and practicing them.

If you are disclosing to request accommodations, depending on when you plan to tell your employers, this will be the most formal type of disclosure you would have to do at work. If you request accommodations for the interview, explain to the employer, or to the person scheduling the interview, what you are requesting. Let them know that you have ASD, and be prepared to explain why the impact of ASD needs to be accommodated. During the interview, it is inappropriate to request formal accommodations for a job you have not yet been offered. You may want to ask what would be available for someone with ASD as part of your disclosure conversation, but save the technicalities of workplace accommodations for a later time, once you have been offered the job. Once you begin working, you will develop a clearer understanding of the role you have and how, if at all, ASD impacts you in the workplace. If you find that you need to request an accommodation or wish to ask questions about your concerns, schedule a meeting with your supervisor and/or HR. Prepare for the meeting by writing down your concerns and practicing any scripts you have developed for disclosing ASD in order to receive accommodations.

Some situations might call for disclosure to explain behavior. This is particularly the case for group projects or when you have to work closely with others. You may need to ask your co-workers for support preparing for a concise presentation at a company-wide gathering, for example, if you have a tendency to become visibly anxious in large groups. You may want to let your desk neighbor know that you wear headphones to help with sensory overload so that they don't assume that you are not available for conversation. Telling others about ASD in these examples should specifically address the behavior, and, when appropriate, imply openness to feedback. When it comes to behavior, if you are acting outside social norms for your workplace, a co-worker may simply ask you about the behavior. If this happens, whether or not you disclose ASD, be open to feedback. Explaining ASD can help others respond more receptively to behavior oddities that may occur at work.

If you are disclosing to share personal information about yourself after having become friends with co-workers, this is the most casual disclosure type. What young adults with ASD should remember in this case are the general unspoken social rules for sharing personal information. First, if you decide to share that you have ASD with co-workers, be mindful of timing. Although your main source of interactions with co-workers is most likely during work time itself, you may have little free time during which to have many personal discussions. Co-worker relationships are developed through proximity and sameness of goals, so with time, you may find yourself eating lunch with co-workers, chatting with them before meetings, or going out after work with them socially. Just as family, hobbies, and interests are likely to become topics of conversation between work friends, the fact that you have ASD may simply be disclosed as part of a conversation about one of your interests. Generally, though, when it comes to telling co-workers about ASD, be aware of your setting and, if in doubt, ask if this would be a good time to talk about something important to you. Again, develop a script for casual disclosure that you may refer to if you find yourself struggling to find the words in the moment.

One more distinction between how people disclose is that it often occurs proactively, and at other times it is reactive. Proactive disclosure is appropriate for situations such as before an interview or to set up accommodations at the start of your work in a new position. Reactive disclosure is when an explanation of ASD is needed to explain a pattern of behavior or to ask for social cue clarification, for example. While both types are valid and used for various situations in the workplace, be mindful of your demeanor and approach to disclosure if it occurs reactively. Individuals with ASD may react impulsively and disclose ASD out of context or at a socially inappropriate time. Pause, and remember your plan for disclosure; if possible, wait for an appropriate time and be prepared with a script that you have practiced in advance.

LESSON 3: TELL YOUR OWN STORY

When it comes to disclosing something important about yourself to those around you, recognize that you cannot control their responses. Unfortunately, many people still have misconceptions about ASD. So if you consider disclosure in your future career, be aware of potential reactions so you are not caught off guard. Sharing information can lead others to have more questions. Answer their questions as much as you are comfortable. Being able to tell your own story is a way to educate others about ASD and to relate to many others around you. Your experiences and interests may resonate with someone in the workplace and lead to friendships and even opportunities for professional growth and career advancement.

ASD can mean many things to all kinds of people who are associated with it, either by their own diagnosis, or that of someone they care about. As the impact is different across the spectrum and between individuals, experiences regarding ASD may share common themes, but are generally specific to individuals. Because of this variation in impact, it is important that you avoid letting your experience be defined by others based on their perception of and familiarity with ASD. If you don't tell your own story, other people may fill in the blanks you've not shared with them, and their perceptions may cause them to have wrong ideas about who you are and what you need as a person with ASD.

BEN'S STORY

Ben applied for a part-time position at a law firm near his college campus. The job description read as follows:

WANTED

Part-time paralegal for an established downtown law firm. Must have valid driver's license and reliable transportation. Duties include but may not be limited to: ability to establish rapport with clients, perform legal and factual research, identify relevant judicial decisions, statements, legal articles, codes and other pertinent material, keen ability to organize and analyze information, cross-check and validate information, prepare well written reports free of grammatical errors, review and monitor new and updated laws and regulations, coordinate law office activities such as subpoena delivery, make deliveries as required to courts and offices daily.

FIGURE 3.2 AN EXAMPLE OF A JOB ADVERTISEMENT

In the job description it clearly states that he is expected to greet clients, answer general calls, and run paperwork around town as needed. Ben adjusted his resume, submitted it, and actually got a call to interview at the law firm. After a week of interview preparation he went in, did exceptionally well in the interview, and was offered a part-time job. The requirements for the job include access to transportation, knowledge of the firm's client process, and the ability to engage with clients and potential clients who come to the office. Ben has worked delivery jobs before, so he's familiar with driving for work and enjoys the time alone in the car, but he's never had to approach clients with this level of professionalism. Ben has concerns about the social aspects of the position, and wishes to clarify the parameters of his responsibility to interact with others. During the several days of training he interacted a lot, and actually made a connection with one of the secretaries at the firm. One day he brought up his concerns to the secretary and asked for clarification about social interactions with clients. He talked about how much he was enjoying the job but that sometimes he struggles to understand the level of professionalism to use while interacting with clients. The secretary shared her experiences about her interactions with clients. She helped Ben identify some of the more elite clients, and how over time he would be able to discern which clients he can be more relaxed with.

What are Ben's valid concerns about his new position?

_____

_____

_____

_____

What are some other ways Ben could have disclosed if he had decided to?

_____

_____

_____

_____

What might be the difference between the interactions Ben might have with elite clients versus the clients who are more "laid back"?

_____

_____

_____

_____

SARAH'S STORY

Sarah works as a technical assistant at a pharmaceutical laboratory. She is employed full-time and often works close to 50 hours a week. Her days are busy and long, and she sometimes makes mistakes because she doesn't have time to slow her brain down between experiments in the lab. She knows that if she had an extra day to re-group after the weekend, and instead worked four longer days to still maintain full-time employment status, that she would ultimately be much more productive for the lab. Her employer is kind and approachable, but no one else has a modified work schedule. Sarah knows that she needs to advocate for herself, and has decided to disclose her ASD diagnosis in the hope that her boss will accommodate her need for extra time to process information, and offer her a longer break so she makes fewer mistakes. She emails her boss requesting his availability for the upcoming week, and asks if he would be available for a meeting.

During the meeting with her boss Sarah discusses how much she loves the job but was honest about some of the mistakes she had been making in the lab. She assured him that she had gone back and caught her own mistakes, and that the issues had been resolved, but wanted to talk through what she thinks might be happening. She explained how excited she was that business had picked up, and that more and more projects were hosted in the lab, but stated that she was having a hard time starting a project and having to hand it over mid-way through, starting two new projects the following day. She went on to say that she had been diagnosed several years ago with ASD, and explained both the strengths and weaknesses of the impact ASD has on her ability to process information. She had thought long and hard about disclosing because she didn't want to use it as an excuse or to alter the company's expectations of her ability or her performance. Her boss was really encouraging and appreciated her bringing up the mistakes that she was making, and acknowledged Sarah as a contributing member of the team and even asked how administration could help her in accommodating the fast-paced environment. Sarah proposed that she work longer days and have the extra day off each week to give her the ability to start and finish the same project, and the extra day would give her time to wind down each week. Sarah's boss agreed to grant her request on a temporary basis and to re-evaluate the arrangement in six months time. Sarah agreed, and was assured that if this didn't work, they would do what they could to accommodate her needs.

What potentially impacted the success of Sarah's performance?

_____

_____

_____

_____

What strengths did Sarah have that made her a good candidate for this job?

_____

_____

_____

_____

What are some other ways Sarah could have advocated for herself had the boss been less understanding?

_____

_____

_____

_____

LAUREN'S STORY

Lauren was recently hired as a full-time employee at the federal university. After two weeks at her new job as executive assistant for a university administrator, her boss gave her some informal feedback. He chided her for her tendency to forget the important details of the daily schedule. He would often walk by her office and say things on his to do list for Lauren to do, which included appointment times and upcoming meetings. She made notes but often missed the important details, such as time and place. She knew this was causing frustration on the part of her boss and those with whom he was expected to meet. He would often show up at the wrong room or at the wrong time, all due to Lauren's incorrect notes of his verbal scheduling reminders.

In college, Lauren had accommodations that included the use of a smart pen during her lectures. The pen recorded the speaker and allowed her to quickly go back to replay parts of the lecture she had missed when distracted. She wanted to use a smart pen, but wasn't sure how her boss would feel about her recording his conversations. She wasn't sure if she would have to disclose that she has ASD and sometimes needs extra time to process important details given in conversation.

What might Lauren say so that these issues are brought up for her boss's attention?

_____

_____

_____

_____

What strategies could Lauren take if she decided not to disclose to her boss?

_____

_____

_____

_____

What would you consider to be the ideal outcome for Lauren?

_____

_____

_____

_____

LESSON 4: PROFESSIONAL TOOL FOR NAVIGATING DISCLOSURE

When young adults with ASD enter the workforce, knowing the right place, the right time, and the right way to disclose can be complicated. Disclosure, because of its tendency to be complicated and lacking a defined set of absolute steps, is a "gray area" young professionals with ASD will encounter (Rigler *et al.* 2015b). While there is no one absolute way to tell others about ASD or to advocate for accommodation needs as an individual with ASD, having a plan for if, when, how, and to whom you will disclose can ease a lot of stress. Being mindful of your legal protections and considering the possible implications of discussing ASD at work are your responsibility as a young adult in your career.

Not everyone will choose to disclose; some with ASD interview for, obtain, and maintain positions for long periods of time without ever telling anyone at work that they have ASD. Disclosing ASD is not always a good idea, especially if it is done impulsively in an inappropriate social context or as an attempt to offer an explanation for poor work behavior that has nothing to do with the impact of ASD. But for those who do disclose to seek support or simply to share personal information with co-workers, the steps involved in assessing why, when, and how to disclose depend on their own unique situation and the impact of ASD for them at work. To understand the distinctions between legal, professional, and personal disclosure and how they influence a disclosure plan, refer to the following descriptions for each of the three types. Then, using the disclosure models (see below) for guidance, consider the example situations and how you could navigate disclosure for each, if at all.

- **Legal disclosure:** Telling employers about ASD in order to establish reasonable workplace accommodations or to gain legal protection from disability-involved discrimination.

- **Professional disclosure:** Telling co-workers about ASD to explain your need/ desire for their informal support, to seek clarification, and to explain behavior.

- **Personal disclosure:** Sharing your experiences with ASD through an interpersonal interaction with no expectation other than conversation and to establish friendships.

DISCLOSURE MODELS

Consider these hypothetical situations that could arise in your future workplace. The arrows connecting the boxes could be potential indicators for whether you should consider disclosing an ASD diagnosis or not.

Consider your response to disclosure using the models for the following prompts:

Once a month your department practices fire drills. The fire alarms are very loud and are accompanied by flashing lights.

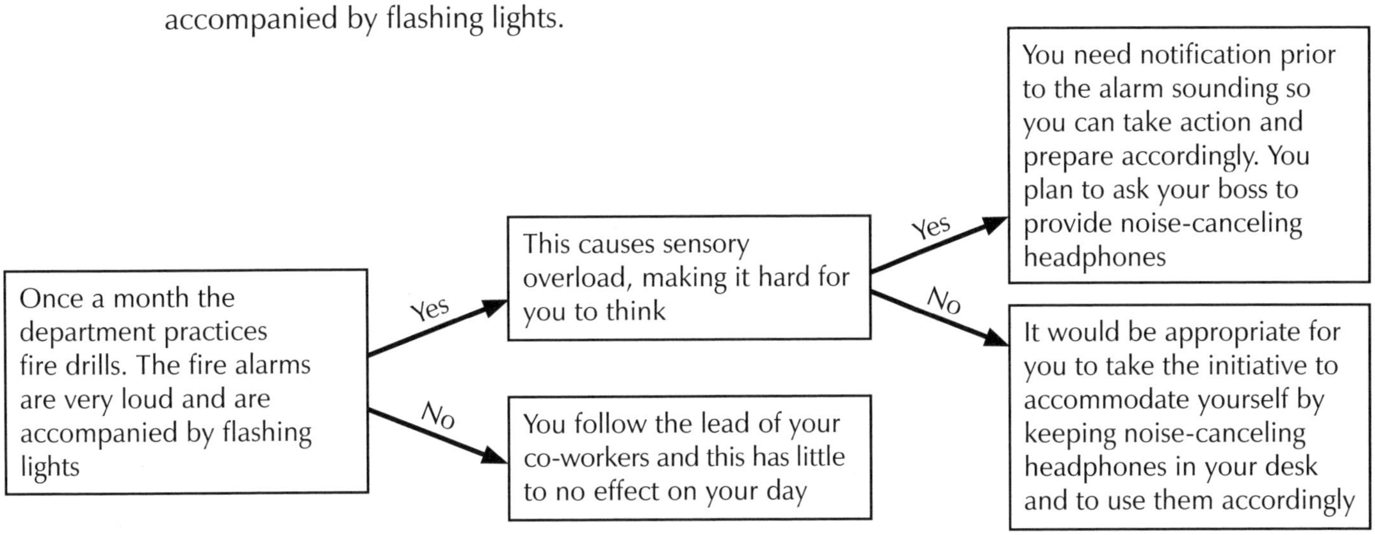

FIGURE 3.3 DISCLOSURE PROMPT 1

Disclose: Yes ☐ No ☐

What potential disclosure type is this? **Legal** ☐ **Professional** ☐ **Personal** ☐

If yes, **when** could you tell someone and **how**?

_____

_____

_____

You have been staying up late and have overslept every morning this week, causing you to be 20 minutes late to work three times.

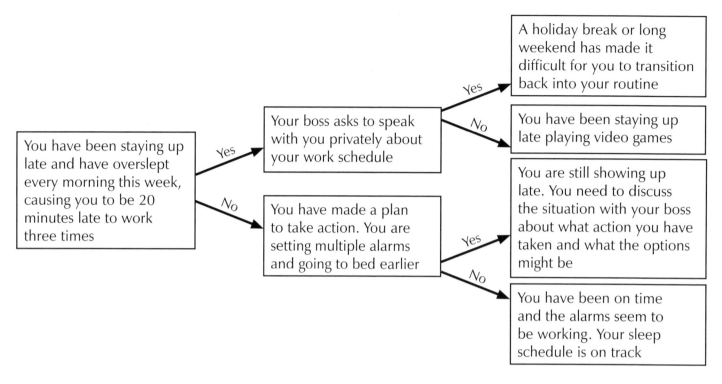

FIGURE 3.4 DISCLOSURE PROMPT 2

Disclose: Yes ☐ No ☐

What potential disclosure type is this? **Legal** ☐ **Professional** ☐ **Personal** ☐

If yes, **when** could you tell someone and **how**?

_____

_____

_____

You've been sharing your lunch break with Jason for several weeks and consider him a friend.

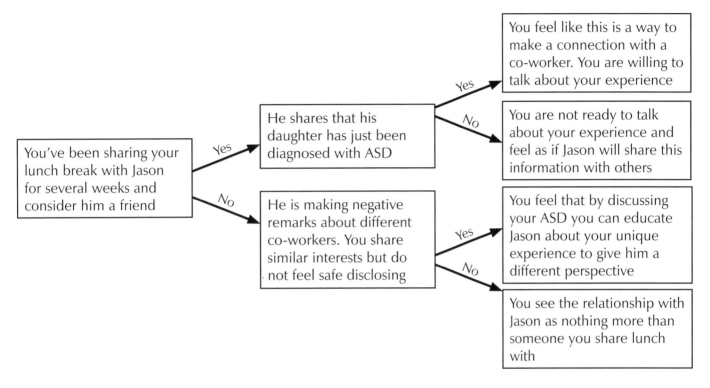

FIGURE 3.5 DISCLOSURE PROMPT 3

Disclose: Yes ☐ No ☐

What potential disclosure type is this? **Legal** ☐ **Professional** ☐ **Personal** ☐

If yes, **when** could you tell someone and **how**?

_____

_____

_____

While these three situations offer guidance as you become familiar with the disclosure models, your own experiences and needs as an individual with ASD will determine how they can be used in your future career. Legal protections are set in place to ensure equal access for and to prohibit discrimination against individuals with disabilities in the workplace. Seeking support under this legal protection, sharing personal information, and explaining behavior are some valid reasons to disclose ASD in the workplace.

Use this professional tool to consider how disclosure is best directed so you can take ownership of your work environment and tasks, so you are the most effective employee you can be.

BACK TO BASICS

B Behavior 1 2 3	Are you focusing on your strengths? Will disclosure have an impact on your career choice? Do you have a plan in case your disclosure is not well received? Are you self-advocating?
A Academics 1 2 3	Do you plan on requesting accommodations? Will it emphasize your strengths if you disclose? Will disclosing help you meet the essential requirements of your job?
S Self-care 1 2 3	Are you sleeping? Are you eating healthily? Are you staying mindful of personal and professional boundaries? Are you maintaining appropriate hygiene? Are you monitoring your concerns regarding disclosure?
I Interaction 1 2 3	Do you have a plan to approach your supervisor to disclose? Do you feel as if disclosure will affect your communication style? Are you aware of the disability culture at work? Are you mindful of the impact of other people's disabilities at work?
C Community 1 2 3	Are you consulting with those you trust regarding disclosure in the workplace? Are you able to envision an ideal outcome in your workplace if you choose to disclose? Do you feel like you are contributing to diversity in the workplace?
S Self-monitoring 1 2 3	Can you identify any benefits in disclosing your ASD? Can you identify any benefits in non-disclosure? Are you able to see yourself overcoming the barriers that stand in the way of your career goals? Do you have realistic expectations?

GOALS

Personal:

Aptitude:

Social:

⬇ BACK TO BASICS: RATE YOURSELF

B	**Behavior** 1 2 3	**Comments**
A	**Academics** 1 2 3	**Comments**
S	**Self-care** 1 2 3	**Comments**
I	**Interaction** 1 2 3	**Comments**
C	**Community** 1 2 3	**Comments**
S	**Self-monitoring** 1 2 3	**Comments**

GOALS

Personal:

Aptitude:

Social:

Chapter 4

PROFESSIONAL WORKPLACE STRUCTURE

INTRODUCTION

Professional communication involves more than discussing work procedures; it involves communication with peers as well as reporting directly to a supervisor about work progress. While some individuals with ASD may prefer such a level of social interaction and communication, it is unrealistic to expect a minimal amount of social interaction and communication. The workplace is the context for a multitude of social situations during which small talk is unavoidable, meaningful participation in discussion is encouraged, and successful interpretation of verbal and non-verbal cues is expected.

Young adults with ASD in college can prepare for many workplace situations by learning self-advocacy skills and practicing professional communication strategies. Developing these communication tools can be achieved through both formal and informal interactions with university staff and through engagement in primarily social and peer-based organizations or activities. Transforming these useable skills to the workplace involves assessing contexts and understanding often-unwritten workplace relationship dynamics.

In preparing for the workplace, you will first need to be aware of and able to identify the levels of professional status of the people with whom you will work. Understanding where people are in terms of social status in the workplace is important because communication and social engagement expectations will differ depending on professional status. Simply put, positional hierarchy in the workplace determines the appropriate social interaction and communication method.

The layers of communication you should anticipate at work vary from casual and personal to professional and strictly business-related. Having a basic idea of how a common workplace social structure is set up will prepare individuals with ASD for communicating effectively.

In addition to recognizing the professional layers in the workplace, you will need to adopt communication strategies to apply during interactions with professionals at all status levels. This involves assessing the physical environment, the culture of the workplace, and people's non-verbal cues to determine the best method of communication. Essential conversations, especially about job expectations, are the responsibility of both employers and employees. Being able to provide input, to offer and receive feedback, and to seek clarification demands that strategies for communication are considered comprehensively for individuals with ASD.

Employers and employees consider factors such as job expectations, awareness of productivity requirements, and access to support at work to be markers of a successful employment arrangement (Scott *et al.* 2015). Miscommunication regarding these factors can lead to serious consequences that impact both employees and their employers. Since keeping positions filled with skilled workers is a priority for employers, and having a job is a priority for employees, communication, especially about expectations (work and social), to maintain employment retention, is therefore a shared responsibility (Scott *et al.* 2015). Knowing that communication and social barriers are often present, young adults with ASD must pay careful attention to matters of employment expectations.

LESSON 1: UNDERSTANDING PROFESSIONAL COMMUNICATION

Workplace social structure can be especially confusing for someone on the spectrum who likely views work as just that—work (Simone 2010). But in contrast, neurotypical employees typically approach their work through a social lens. Their actions and reactions are driven by social motives in the workplace, despite the fact that it fundamentally exists as a space for production and work. Individuals with ASD in the workplace have a tendency to hit a glass ceiling (Fast 2004), which means that despite all other skills and qualifications, unmitigated social miscues can make it exceptionally difficult for someone on the spectrum to transition to higher professional status levels. Thus, awareness of professional status levels and how they influence social behavior is essential.

While neurotypical employees may be more intrinsically attuned to this notion, employees with ASD will need guidance in this area. Professional status levels determine why communication expectations with a boss differ from that with an assistant, for example. In many cases social status levels in the workplace are tied to positions. While lower levels of employment such as part-time assistants or interns may have access to explicit guidelines for communication and social engagement, as social status increases at work, the unspoken social nuances become subtler and therefore harder to read for those with ASD (Fast 2004; Meyer 2001). Preparing for this unspoken workplace social order should help you to avoid some common pitfalls.

FIVE PROFESSIONAL STATUS LEVELS

Further complicating the task of learning professional communication strategies is the fact that professional status levels may have varying definitions and characteristics depending on the culture of an individual workplace. Generally, though, consider where the people with whom you work would fall within a common professional status hierarchy. Again, not all employees fall easily into one of these categorized levels. Bissonnette (2013) contends there are actually two organizational charts in every company: one is an official chart, showing supervision and employee reporting guidelines, while the second is an informal organization chart. Sometimes the two align and parallel one another, but the unwritten and informal chart can offer more meaningful information to an individual with ASD who is working toward understanding communication strategies at work. Removing the guesswork in learning how to adapt communication styles and behavior in response to the status level of those with whom you work can be done by assessing professional status based on the five defined levels, as shown below.

Table 4.1 The five professional status levels

Professional status level	Common characteristics	Example positions
LEVEL FIVE	Individuals in leadership positions responsible for overseeing all operations of a workplace	*Organizational leadership:* chief executive officers, company presidents
LEVEL FOUR	Individuals in supervisory position with high levels of responsibility and leadership	*Divisional leadership:* department directors, vice presidents, regional managers
LEVEL THREE	Individuals in roles with significant responsibility and some supervisory/ leadership involvement	*Mid-level professionals:* managers, assistant directors
LEVEL TWO	Employees fully and professionally engaged, but with limited responsibility and leadership	*Entry-level professional:* technicians, specialists, coordinators
LEVEL ONE	Employees working in part-time, often temporary, support roles	*Support staff:* assistants, interns, volunteers

As college students, communicating effectively begins with recognizing that the way you speak with and interact with your close friends is usually different from the way you communicate with your professors.

As a young professional, you will likely enter the workplace in a Level One position, which is a great context for learning the social nuances of a workplace, but this means that you will need to quickly assess your co-workers in the social environment and take note of their professional interactions.

Ask yourself these questions about your workplace's social environment:

- How do your co-workers greet you and one another?

- Who is responsible for the work that directly relates to yours?

- Does anyone do the same or a very similar job that you do?

- How do others at a similar professional level as you address other co-workers?

- Is there a pattern in your co-workers' tendency to gather and chat socially?

- How do your co-workers communicate with you outside of work hours for social reasons? Is it common for co-workers to exchange personal cell phone numbers?

- What types of questions are asked via email? What types of questions are asked in scheduled and structured formal meetings?

- Who attends regular work meetings? What is your role at these meetings?

- Which co-worker manages scheduling and general office questions?

- Do co-workers refer to each other by first name or by title and last name?

- How do your same level co-workers greet you? How do they greet individuals in higher or lower professional status positions?

- Which co-workers are in leadership positions?

- Does the office have any part-time, support staff members?

- To what extent are you expected to participate in voluntary post-work social events?

On the one hand, the responses to these questions can help you navigate the social environment at your workplace by allowing you to situate co-workers within a context of defined, predictable, professional status levels. These five levels aim to represent a standard workplace social structure, which, for a young adult with ASD, is an organizational tool for understanding the essential, yet often unwritten, context for demonstrating appropriate communication strategies. The levels are practical designations for common social expectations between individuals of varying professional status in the workplace.

Most common social settings involve such a structure, and college is an especially similar one. Just as you would not send a flippant text message to an instructor as you would to a classmate or friend, in the professional world, communicating with someone in a higher professional status level by means of an unscheduled, casual office visit would not be appropriate. Similarly, as a young professional in a Level One position, you would not greet someone in a Level Five leadership role by his or her first name as you might someone with whom you work on a daily basis who is also in a Level One position. These distinctions, while they are not overtly designed in the workplace to demand special communication consideration, can help individuals with ASD process the structure of the social environment at work.

One the other hand, you may find that there is little variation in communication patterns regarding the professional status levels identified here. It is possible that a leader such as a chief executive officer (Level Five) may, in fact, prefer to be greeted personally by his first name by all employees, which is no different than the part-time student intern's preference (Level One).

Unpredictable variations in how unwritten professional status levels practically impact communication can be challenging for all young professionals to interpret. Experience and feedback will guide your social transition to the workplace. As you adjust to the new work environment, be especially mindful of patterns in social interactions and communication styles with all of your co-workers and those in leadership positions.

OFFICE POLITICS

Another way to describe these professional social structures at the workplace is "office politics." Bissonnette (2013, p.78) describes office politics as "the unspoken rules about who has power in an organization, and how things get done." While neurotypical employees who are more socially inclined will likely find value in the concept of office politics, those with ASD are likely to consider office politics to be complicated. Unfortunately, for those with ASD, office politics is an unavoidable concept—knowing who has authority for making things happen at work is imperative.

The official type of organization chart that outlines professional positions, to whom each position reports, is generally discussed during a new employee's training and transition period. But the other type of organization chart, outlining where the power lies unofficially, will not be available as such. You should therefore pay specific attention to the unspoken rules and power structure within a workplace.

Consider a few examples of office politics to gain an idea of the social situations you may encounter, such as the hiring of an applicant based on an employer's bias (e.g., the applicant is the provost's daughter, but is otherwise unqualified, or the applicant graduated from the same college). Another example would be the promotion of an employee based on favoritism. The appointment and set-up of committees and decision-making boards is another aspect of the workplace that may be political. While some degree of office politics will likely be part of the social culture at your workplace, overt political or biased actions in the workplace are generally discouraged. It will take some time to understand how the social environment of your workplace influences its operations. Office politics rarely make sense to those who are not directly involved, and certainly may appear unfair to those impacted at the workplace. Once you gain an idea of the social structure of the workplace, you will be more aware of office politics, and how they influence the work environment.

Taking the time to assess the social structure and communication expectations at any workplace is a necessary element of successful transition. While it may be frustrating to confront the social conventions influencing how you are expected to communicate and participate socially at work, it is important that you avoid obsessing over determining professional status levels and understanding the particulars of office politics. The five levels outlined in this chapter are generalizations; your workplace professional status levels may be outlined differently based on your workplace's individual social culture and the preferences of the professionals in various positions. Observing communication patterns and modeling professional communication is something that all young professionals are tasked with in a new position.

When in doubt about how to approach a social situation at work, consult with a co-worker who has experience at your workplace. It is not inappropriate or uncommon for new professionals to ask for such social guidance at work. But be mindful of your co-worker's time, and use discretion, note their responses, and consider their advice as it applies to your dilemma, and avoid asking the same questions multiple times.

You can learn a lot about the social expectations of your workplace by asking questions, keeping note of responses, and by modeling those in similar positions as they interact with others at work.

LESSON 2: COMMUNICATION STRATEGIES

After individuals with ASD have a solid grasp on the social structure of the workplace, including how office politics influence processes and how communication expectations vary based on work culture and the influence of professional status levels, the next step is to identify areas for applying practical communication strategies. Part of the challenge for young professionals, especially those with ASD, is that communication in the workplace has unwritten and unspoken guidelines, and failing to recognize them can lead to social confusion and embarrassing miscues. In addition to simple one-on-one verbal conversation, body language, physical layout of the workplace, and the use of technology-based mobile devices are involved in workplace communication.

Your employer's expectations will be conveyed in many ways, and it is your responsibility to maintain communication with your employer for any of your concerns. Practical application of communication strategies occurs through proactive measures and reactive responses. Paying attention to details, being resourceful and creative problem solvers, and adhering to structure when it is established are likely to be the strengths of young professionals with ASD. And these strengths can be used to navigate the professional communication interactions within and across professional status levels at work.

Specific workplace aspects such as the number of employees, how much customer/client contact is expected, and even the physical workplace set-up are matters that impact communication (Meyer 2001). If your workplace employs a smaller number of people, it is more likely to be a casual social environment. On the other hand, as employee numbers increase, it is likely that there will be more structural elements to the social environment due to the different layers of professional statuses. Similarly, consider how often you are expected to work in collaboration with others, or if you will spend your time working on projects alone. If you are expected to greet and work with clients or customers, there is another level of social interaction for which you will need to prepare. If this is the case, pay attention to how other people in the same or similar positions as the one you hold interact with clients/customers. Some professional fields have guidelines that will offer support for you in these social contexts.

The way your work setting is physically set up will also influence the social nature of your workplace. An open, cubicle-style office setting will encourage more socialization than, for example, a workplace with individual, closed offices. These clues will help you gauge the social expectations of your workplace as you begin your work. Take note of the company size, likelihood of collaborative projects, and the structure of your workspace to gather information about your workplace's social environment.

Another element of professional communication that individuals with ASD will need to consider as they prepare for the professional social structure of the workplace is body language. The unspoken communication that occurs through people's body language can have just as much influence as their words. Your body language in the workplace speaks for you as early as the first greeting at an interview. Your ability to maintain eye contact, initiate a handshake, or demonstrate genuine interest in a co-worker's conversation with you is paramount. In college, you had to be aware of how your body language was perceived by your instructors and peers in order to successfully navigate the campus' social maze. Similarly, the workplace is a setting that requires the same, if not more, effort to monitor what your body language says for you.

TOPICS OF CONVERSATION

Body language is not the only specific aspect of communication that should be considered in relation to employment. There is an important distinction between casual, or social, and formal, or work-based, topics of conversation. During lunch or coffee breaks, before and after work, and at after-work social events, casual conversations will be appropriate. Topics for casual conversation vary widely—you could discuss personal interests, community news, current events, and other non-work related themes. On the other hand, on-the-clock hours (scheduled work time) should generally only include formal conversations about work. During work time you should limit your conversations to productive work-related discussions and inquiries. Not every single conversation during your work time will be formal, of course, and you may discuss formal work-related topics while at an after-work social event. Generally, though, and especially until you figure out more about the social nature of the workplace, it is important for you to develop these casual and formal boundaries in topics of conversation.

Young adults with ASD need to prepare for the impact of technology on workplace communication. Verbal speech, body language, and, increasingly, tech-based interaction are all co-requisites for mastering professional communication. As a young professional, you will be expected to understand the social nuances of emailing, texting, videoconferencing, social media, and scheduling through computer-based applications. Many of these technological communication methods allow users to interpret, process, and analyze received communication and to respond after consideration of social cues and appropriate wording. This affects individuals with ASD by allowing for a more structured and efficient exchange of information, through which those with ASD tend to thrive and demonstrate their strengths.

You will need to review, model, and practice professional communication through email, as this is likely to be a fundamental workplace communication tool. Texting and social media, because they are also personal communication tools, should be approached cautiously with co-workers, as they may not be appropriate methods of communication. While you may not use videoconferencing, it would be wise to develop a professional videoconferencing-capable profile with Skype, Zoom, Google Hangouts or any other videoconferencing application just in case this method of communication is requested by a potential employer as the interview medium or used in client meetings, committee gatherings, or presentations with individuals in different locations. Similarly, everyone in your workplace may not use shared computer-based calendars, but programs such as Microsoft Outlook and Google Calendar are useful for scheduling meetings, both work and social, using a structured and common platform.

Scott *et al.* (2015) summarize the need for professional social awareness for professionals with ASD, noting that when employees and employers reach a common ground in matters of job requirements, urgency of task completion, training in work processes and structure, and agree on the availability of resources, the environment is more suited for individuals with ASD. Further, Scott *et al.* (2015) found that employees and employers both have expectations that, when unclear, can result in employees who lack motivation and fail to meet performance standards, an increase in stress, and a decrease in employee retention. As a young professional entering the workplace, it is crucial that expectations are clearly communicated and responsibilities defined. This dialogue should continue with feedback and evaluation throughout progress in a certain position or within a company over time.

Once the elements of a workplace's professional structure are established and an organization chart is explored, the foundation of the culture can be identified and social rules set.

LESSON 3: NAVIGATING PROFESSIONAL MISCUES

Communication blunders at work due to missing social cues, even through they can be embarrassing, are rarely so impactful that they threaten a person's job. While some professional miscues are more consequential than others, not all professional cultures are outright unforgiving of them, however. Young adults with ASD may misunderstand, or simply miss altogether, workplace professional structure and communication cues, and end up in a difficult position socially. Even neurotypical young professionals can benefit from knowing how to respond to professional miscues at work.

Remember that the degree to which some of these miscues impact the young adult's status at work varies, so it is important to think about a response plan if social miscues occur.

The first step in navigating a miscue is, of course, recognizing the social rule you missed. Then, assess how others respond. Consider whether they laugh it off or have taken offense by looking for cues in their body language and any verbal responses. If you have offended them, or need to clarify your meaning or intention, this conversation will be a personal one, and one for which you should prepare.

Take a look at these scenarios involving young adults with ASD having to navigate professional miscues.

HEATHER'S STORY

Heather accepted a position in a large multi-specialty medical group that was staffed with over 25 doctors. During orientation, it was stressed to the new employees not to interfere with other patient care outside their practice. The employee would report only to the assigned practitioner, in Heather's situation, a pediatrician.

However, one day, during a patient emergency, an orthopedic surgeon asked Heather to assist with the care of an elderly patient with a broken hip. Remembering her orientation, Heather ignored the request and continued her break. Not picking up on non-verbal cues, such as the looks of shock on co-workers' faces and others staring and rolling their eyes, she returned to her station and continued to perform her assigned duties. She was then asked to meet with her supervisor and to explain her actions. Heather was shocked to learn that the doctor was furious with her.

What confused Heather in this situation?

_____

_____

_____

_____

How could Heather have managed this situation better?

_____

_____

_____

_____

What could the doctor have said to clarify his request?

_____

_____

_____

_____

AARON'S STORY

The social activities calendar at Aaron's workplace is demanding. The staff are young, enjoy nightlife and a large part of the company's work discussion takes place in a social setting. Attendance at happy hour is expected, and decisions seem to be made based on bonds formed through these social gatherings: the marketing director's trivia night partner was promoted to a leadership position even though he had less experience than others. Marketing assistant Aaron is tired, needs more time to process social cues than is available in a sensory-overloaded bar, and to prepare for the effort it takes to go out so often. Since Aaron has had to miss out on these social activities, he finds it hard to engage with co-workers. He finds out that the marketing director's son is a friendly intern where he takes his dog to the vet for routine exams. He thinks he can use his casual relationship with the son to build a social connection with the marketing director, but isn't sure how to approach it, and is considering just avoiding it altogether.

How could this social connection help Aaron's career?

_____

_____

_____

_____

How can Aaron initiate this connection?

_____

_____

_____

_____

What is the first thing Aaron should say to start this conversation?

_____

_____

_____

_____

HANNAH'S STORY

A highly sought after client at Hannah's architecture firm, Mr. James, refers to Hannah by her first name in casual settings. He does so in their personal offices and when around close mutual co-workers. Hannah and Mr. James worked together for several weeks developing a wish list for his new project using each other's first name in an informal situation. However, because of Mr. James' influential status as a client of Hannah's firm, everyone in her office, including the senior architect, refers to him by Mr. James, and not by his first name, Brad. When Mr. James introduces Hannah's proposal to his company's investment team, he refers to Hannah by her last name in his introduction, setting the tone for a professional presentation. When Hannah begins to present, she blurts out "Thanks, Brad," and is met with mutterings and snickers throughout the conference room.

What could this social miscue tell the others in the room about their relationship?

_____

_____

_____

_____

How could Hannah have remedied this social miscue at the time?

_____

_____

_____

_____

How did Hannah become confused in this situation?

_____

_____

_____

_____

LESSON 4: PROFESSIONAL TOOL FOR MANAGING WORKPLACE COMMUNICATION

When it comes to understanding the professional structure of the workplace, an organization chart can help you see the big picture of the professional statuses of your co-workers. It will also allow you to consider where you would be positioned on the chart, and where others are in relation to you.

Recall the five professional status levels outlined in Lesson One. Take a look at the organization structure chart for an example of how these five levels may be arranged, and read the information on the corresponding cards for each level, to see social and professional progression.

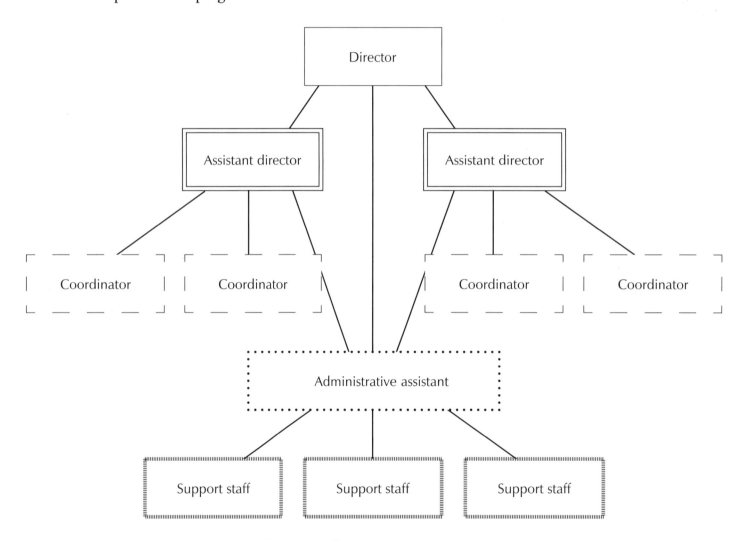

FIGURE 4.1 ORGANIZATION STRUCTURE CHART

Level Five position

Organizational leadership professional:

- Supervises all Level Four professionals directly, and holds leadership with all professionals on staff
- Position demands highest level of responsibility for all workplace operations, including policy development and decision-making, the maintenance of facilities, interference in staff conflicts, and the supervision of all professionals
- Reputable leadership skills, illustrated overall success of the workplace and production, and continued social fit are essential for further highest-level professional status
- Non-work interactions will likely be limited to same level professionals, or Level Four professionals. Rare social interaction may occur with professionals in Levels Three, Two and One positions

Level Four position

Divisional leadership professional:

- Supervised by Level Five professionals
- Positions are leadership roles with a large amount of responsibility, typically including the management of day-to-day operations and supervision of support staff
- Innovative ideas with worthwhile applications, established commitment and personal investment in the workplace, and continued social fit are considered for next level professional advancement
- Non-work social interactions will likely be limited to same level professionals or Levels Three or Five professionals. Social interaction with Levels One and Two professionals will occur only occasionally

Level Three position

Mid-level professional:

- Supervised by Level Four professionals
- Positions often demand relevant experience prior to employment and some demonstrated supervisory experience
- Excellence on all work projects, the development of leadership qualities, and continued social fit are considered for next level professional advancement
- Non-work social interaction with Level One is limited, but likely with Levels Two and Four professionals

Level Two position

Entry-level professional:

- Supervised by Level Three professionals
- Positions require some work experience and professional interest in the employment field
- Aptitude on work projects, demonstrated understanding of the position's responsibilities, and continued social fit are considered for next level professional advancement

Level One position

Support staff:

- Supervised by Level Two professionals
- Positions are often part-time and/or temporary and will have limited responsibility
- Consistency in behavior and work production, a desire and willingness to learn, and social fit are considered for next level professional advancement
- Limited non-work social interaction with Level Two professionals may occur

 Now, in the space below, draw the organizational chart related to your position, if you are employed. If you are not yet in the workplace, think about the organizational chart in relation to any campus organization or club of which you have been a member. You could also do some research about the ideal company that interests you, and outline how you suspect the organization chart of the company is structured, paying attention to staff titles and information about the team from the company website.

Understanding the professional structure of a workplace can alleviate the pressure of avoiding social miscues at work. Once you are aware of the social interaction norms at work, you will be less likely to misinterpret appropriate behavior and communication. Later, in Chapter 7 you will learn specific communication strategies for engaging socially with co-workers at all levels.

BACK TO BASICS

B 1 2 3	**Behavior**	Are you aware of the behavior expectations in your place of employment? Are you mindful of others? Do you respect the various levels identified in the workplace?
A 1 2 3	**Academics**	Are your strengths a fit in the workplace? Do you use your skills set appropriately? Are you attentive to detail?
S 1 2 3	**Self-care**	Are you sleeping? Are you maintaining a healthy diet? Are you staying active? Are you maintaining appropriate hygiene? Are you maintaining a professional image?
I 1 2 3	**Interaction**	Do you practice appropriate communication skills? Have you developed trusting relationships within the workplace? Do you socialize with co-workers on occasion? Are you mindful of your body language and communication style?
C 1 2 3	**Community**	Are you networking? Are you aware of the social and professional culture in your professional setting? Do you monitor your conversation topics?
S 1 2 3	**Self-monitoring**	Do you adhere to a healthy routine? Do you maintain a level of professionalism? Are you mindful of what you put on social media? Are you continuing to self-advocate?

GOALS

Personal:

Aptitude:

Social:

BACK TO BASICS: RATE YOURSELF

B	**Behavior** 1 2 3	Comments
A	**Academics** 1 2 3	Comments
S	**Self-care** 1 2 3	Comments
I	**Interaction** 1 2 3	Comments
C	**Community** 1 2 3	Comments
S	**Self-monitoring** 1 2 3	Comments

GOALS

Personal:

Aptitude:

Social:

Chapter 5

STRESS MANAGEMENT

INTRODUCTION

The transition to life as a new professional can be stressful and overwhelming. Young professionals are expected to use their skills sets very differently in the workplace, often in a new environment or with new people, and must be prepared for the challenges that are presented. The unknown can be a trigger for additional stress for young professionals with ASD. We define triggers as things that produce stress and anxiety in our lives. Being able to identify stress is essential to success in the workplace and the quality of relationships with co-workers. Once you can identify the impact of stress, learning to manage it should then become a priority.

Although learning to manage stress can be a difficult task for anyone, it is particularly difficult for those with ASD. According to Crum, Salovey and Achor (2013), recognizing symptoms of stress, identifying what causes the stress triggers, developing coping strategies, and controlling the emotional response makes up how we cognitively process stress. Each area can be independent of each other, but it is essential that they all work cohesively when stressful situations arise. It is easy to let the demands of the professional world create additional unnecessary stress without understanding or properly developing coping strategies. Being expected to transition from one task to another multiple times throughout the day could create a sense of unmanageable chaos. Time and task management are very important to being professional and successful in both the personal and professional world. Deadlines can change and projects get added or dropped at a moment's notice. There is also an expectation that you will engage in interactions with co-workers. Being prepared to handle the unexpected problems and changes that occur while navigating the social cues of others is a large part of the professional expectation.

With the proper tools in place, your level of stress and anxiety can be better managed, and in return you will feel less chaotic and more controlled. Understanding your own responsibility to control stress, and how to go about identifying stressors, should create a sense of control that will be an essential tool for new professionals learning stress management techniques. In addition to identifying stressors, it is important to develop stress relief techniques, to communicate about stressors at work, and to take ownership of your reactions to stress.

LESSON 1: UNDERSTANDING RESPONSIBILITIES AND IDENTIFYING STRESSORS

The role that stress and anxiety play in the world of young adults with ASD is often overlooked as they navigate the transition to life as new professionals. It is essential that as you begin your journey as a new professional, that you learn to respect your physical and emotional health.

It can be a difficult task to recognize the reaction and impact that stress has on your body, especially for those with ASD. This is because stress presents itself very differently for each person. Pay attention to these signs, learn to identify symptoms of stress, and develop strategies that will help you seek a reasonable response.

Use the image in Figure 5.1, developed by Rigler *et al.* (2015a), to help you identify how stress feels in the various parts of your own body, and use this as a reference to help prompt when action is required.

Highlight the statements that apply to you during uneasy times. These may not all be attributed to stress, but they can play an important role in identifying and managing the onset of stress.

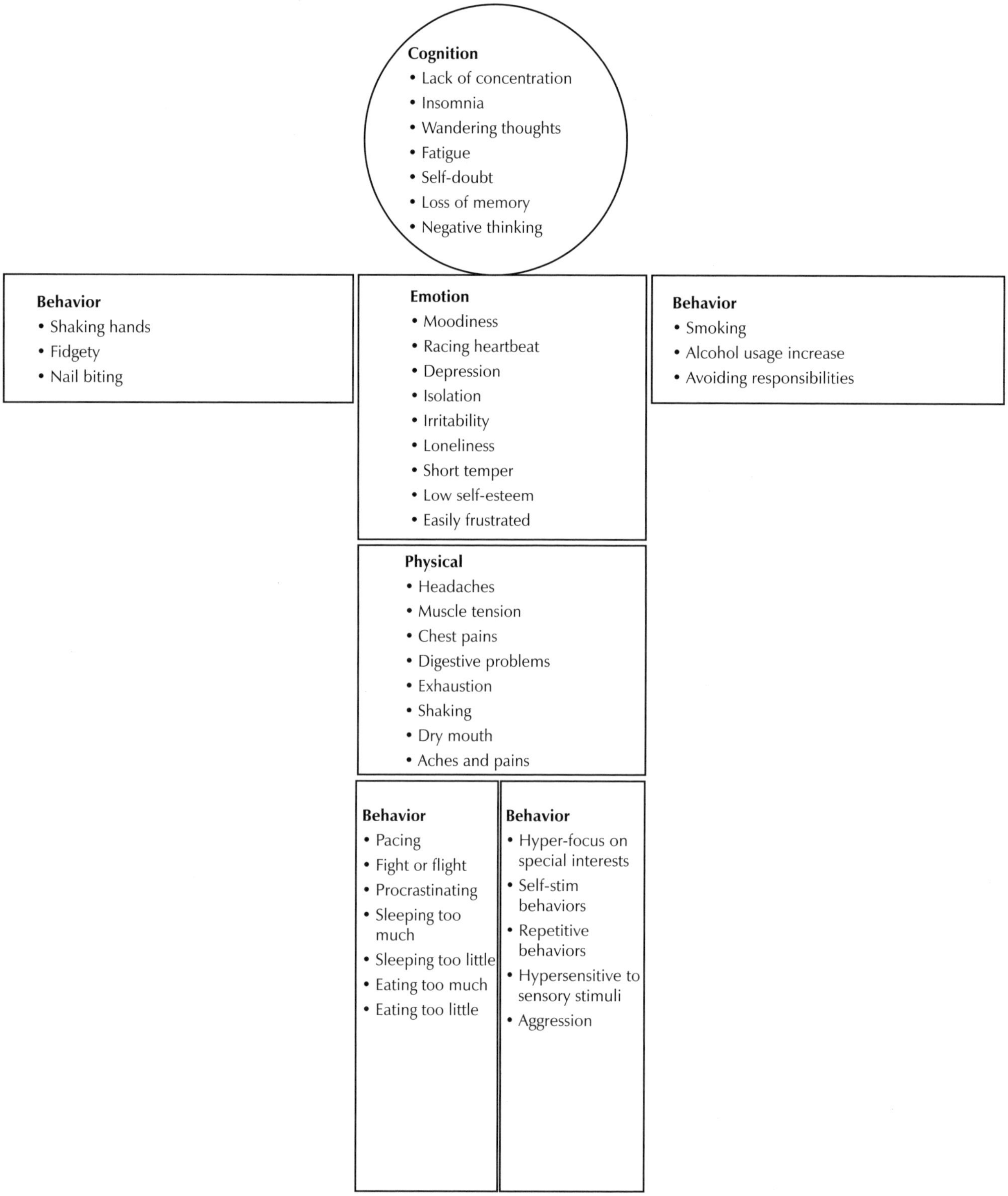

Cognition
- Lack of concentration
- Insomnia
- Wandering thoughts
- Fatigue
- Self-doubt
- Loss of memory
- Negative thinking

Behavior
- Shaking hands
- Fidgety
- Nail biting

Emotion
- Moodiness
- Racing heartbeat
- Depression
- Isolation
- Irritability
- Loneliness
- Short temper
- Low self-esteem
- Easily frustrated

Behavior
- Smoking
- Alcohol usage increase
- Avoiding responsibilities

Physical
- Headaches
- Muscle tension
- Chest pains
- Digestive problems
- Exhaustion
- Shaking
- Dry mouth
- Aches and pains

Behavior
- Pacing
- Fight or flight
- Procrastinating
- Sleeping too much
- Sleeping too little
- Eating too much
- Eating too little

Behavior
- Hyper-focus on special interests
- Self-stim behaviors
- Repetitive behaviors
- Hypersensitive to sensory stimuli
- Aggression

FIGURE 5.1 IDENTIFYING SYMPTOMS OF STRESS

In what ways does stress impact how you think?

_____

_____

_____

_____

How does stress emotionally impact you?

_____

_____

_____

_____

How are your reactions different when you are stressed?

_____

_____

_____

_____

What is something you need to be mindful of when you begin to feel stressed?

_____

_____

_____

_____

Now that you have identified what stress might look and feel like, your responsibility shifts to learning how to understand what triggers your stress, and to use appropriate coping strategies. Essentially, the expectation is for you to take responsibility for controlling your emotional and physical responses to stress. Taking control and implementing healthy coping strategies can help prevent stress escalating to anger, thus potentially preventing stress having a negative impact on you as a professional.

For many professionals, stress comes as part of the job. A project/report deadline, sharing a workspace, concerns about the unknown, little to no direction given for a task, and a last-minute mandatory meeting—these are all examples of common stress triggers that occur in the workplace. Although most professionals share these triggers, individuals with ASD have additional stressors that often get overlooked by neurotypical co-workers and supervisors, such as sensory sensitivities, feelings of failure, unpredictable daily tasks, and misinterpreting social or peer-to-peer interactions. Learning to balance all these things while fulfilling the employer's expectations can help you balance your social energy level and prevent burnout.

As a young professional it is your responsibility to recognize the symptoms, know your triggers, and control your responses and reactions. It is important to take ownership of your stress and to prevent yourself from passing the blame on to others. We define this as "projection," which is one of many defense mechanisms commonly used during heightened times of stress. In Lesson 2 we explore the various types of defense mechanisms and how these might impact you in a professional setting.

It is expected that both young and seasoned professionals monitor their own behavior and recognize the chain of command and professional status levels of co-workers within the workplace. Knowing what makes you feel stress and understanding what can lead to unacceptable behavior will help you maintain control of your behavior, and keep you employed.

Use the following situational stress test to examine what you view as potential stressors in the workplace.

 ## SITUATIONAL STRESS TEST

Rate each of these situations according to how stressful they would be for you personally. Rate each with either "1" for very little stress, "2" for moderate stress, or "3" for very stressful. The items rated as "3" can be seen as your potential stressful triggers.

Situation	Rating	Comment
Your alarm didn't go off, and now you're running late for work		
Your co-workers leave the coffee station in a mess		
You get called to an impromptu meeting		
The seat you usually sit in during staff meetings is taken by someone else		
Your co-workers have a disagreement about a task outside your office		
In the middle of a meeting your pen runs out of ink		

You have to walk through a crowd of people to get to your desk every morning		
You were asked to collaborate with a different department on a project		
A meeting time is changed to a later date		
Your co-worker likes to play music loud enough for you to hear while they work		
You worked really hard on a presentation and now the USB stick is missing from your desk		
Your boss announces a change in the deadline for an upcoming project		
Your friend cancelled plans to go to a movie after work		
Your boss asked you to stay late to finish the project you have been working on		
Two co-workers are conferring outside of your cubicle, and it is distracting you		
Other:		

LESSON 2: MANAGING YOUR ENVIRONMENT

A professional work environment can be a place of constant sensory stimulation that contributes to stress. Frequent interactions with co-workers, shuffling of papers and tasks, distractions via email or phone calls, the flickering of fluorescent lights, and unique smells and sounds are only a few of the challenges you might face daily at work.

Remember that stress is, in fact, a normal part of the professional world. The American Psychological Association (2014) states that everyone who has ever held a job has at some point felt the pressure of work-related stress. Sources for both short-term and long-term triggers for work-related stressors include experiencing pressure to meet a deadline, excessive workload, doing tasks that are not engaging or challenging, lack of social support, and the unpredictability and conflicting demands or unclear expectations of performance (American Psychological Association 2014). Everyone has triggers, which in this context are defined as things, situations, or sensory stimulation, which produce or lead to stress and anxiety in our lives. Give yourself permission to feel stressed, but spend time reflecting on how you should cope, and learn your limits. Even in neurotypical people, tolerance of the stressors in lives can vary from situation to situation. Although stressors can be identified as barriers, if viewed in the proper context, they can be managed if you stick to your strengths.

One aspect to consider as a contributing component of the low stress tolerance experienced by many individuals with ASD is the unpredictable nature of life. We all have ideas of what day-to-day operations should look like, but understanding that situations arise has an effect on our own reaction to those situations—and we can be better prepared to manage the changes.

One notable strength of individuals with ASD is the ability to adhere to and thrive in a routine. When a routine is altered, those with ASD often have difficulty adjusting. If you think about how important it is to be proactive in setting up a stress relief routine, you can begin to explore how the many strengths associated with ASD play a role in managing stress as a new professional. This ability to develop and maintain a routine is essential when it comes to maintaining control of stressors.

Constant stimulation combined with hypersensitivity could lead to sensory overload if not properly managed. Hypersensitivities occur when one of your five senses overloads with too much sensory input, which creates a high level of stress (Rigler *et al.* 2015a). People with ASD often have hyper- or hyposensitivity in one or more of their senses (Attwood 1999).

Another strength common in individuals with ASD is the ability to set and maintain strict personal boundaries. Those with ASD tend to be rule followers, even those rules they set for themselves. When dealing with stress in the workplace, set rules to maintain certain boundaries regarding time spent "chit-chatting," working from home, using your headphones to drown out background noise for at least part of your work day, for example. This will help you to recognize when the stressors begin to take their toll so that you can prevent any negative effects from the stressful situation.

A practical example would be if your supervisor asked you to stay late in order to complete a project. You decline, because a boundary you have set for yourself is to get at least eight hours sleep a night. This decision could have a negative effect on your team members, but represents a positive effect on your well-being. In this type of situation, however, be cautious in regularly declining such requests. You should only really adhere to this rule when your coping ability has reached its limit.

REDUCING STRESS

As you learn to recognize patterns in the elements of the professional world that create stress for you, you will be able to more effectively reduce the impact of this stress. What works for one person may not work for you, however, so it is up to you to take responsibility to identify what situations cause stress for you, and to develop coping strategies to help get you through those times.

There are several methods for reducing stress.

PROFESSIONAL MENTOR

Identify relationships you have with individuals you can consult with if the stress becomes too much for you to manage on your own. A professional mentor can be a great resource for you as you explore triggers, ways to reduce stress as a new professional, or even just need someone to vent to.

EXECUTIVE FUNCTION SKILLS

An often misunderstood and highly impactful area that contributes to extreme stress for many individuals with ASD is referred to as "executive function." Executive function skills include the ability to plan and organize, to sustain motivation during frustrating tasks, to transition from task to task without losing one's place, regulating emotional responses, and storing information in one's short-term memory (Tantam and van Deurzen 2014).

As a professional, you will need to manage many tasks, attend many meetings and appointments, complete tasks to deadlines, and respond to professional emails in a timely manner, all while refraining from engaging in special interest activities and maintaining focus. Difficulty with executive function skills can be a major contributor to heightened stress levels and loss of employment for those with ASD, but these difficulties can be mitigated with some strategies and practice.

TIME MANAGEMENT

One of the most important things to do when you enter the professional world is to create a time management system that works for you. Many have never needed to rely on a planner of any kind to manage daily events, but the transition into the world of work is different. You must maintain appointments, communicate effectively through email, complete tasks by deadlines, and manage work hours, all independently. The only way to do this effectively is to create a planning system that you can practice and master early in your career.

Your planning system could be a traditional paper planner, daily task lists, computer-based calendar, or many of the highly technical planning apps for smart phones, but should be a system that you can commit to using each day. Regardless of the system you choose to use, each day should begin with a review of your planner and end with a follow-up and goal-setting for the next day of work.

TASK COMPLETION

Within any career, the expectation will be for professionals to complete tasks by designated deadlines. Some of these may be long-term projects that could create frustration, and it will be important to develop a strategy to maintain your focus and motivation during these times. A helpful strategy is to create micro-tasks within the larger project. These smaller tasks can be developed on a timeline that has daily deadlines that should lead to full project completion. It might be helpful to write each micro-task on a sticky-note and place the notes on a timeline, with established deadlines. As you complete the daily task toward project completion, take the task off the timeline and throw it away. This also means that you can set up a daily personal reward for completing your goal, which may involve allowing yourself to spend some time engaging in something related to your special interest. While rewarding yourself will help sustain motivation, take care to monitor the appropriateness of the reward in a professional setting as well as the time spent on the rewarding activity.

ORGANIZATIONAL SYSTEMS

An important aspect of successfully completing tasks and engaging in the professional world is to maintain organization and to keep track of everything needed to engage in the activities of your job. As a professional, you must develop a good time management system and work out ways to maintain focus and motivation during long-term projects, but if you are not successful at staying organized and often lose important things, you will find it difficult to be successful in your career. The development of and commitment to a strict organizational system should help diminish any potential negative consequences of losing important items. Color-coding may be beneficial to those with ASD due to the ease of use once developed. By attributing the same color folder, binder, pens, etc. for each project or task, simply gather all the colored items prior to a meeting. But if you choose this strategy, it is vital to fully commit to it so that the colors maintain purpose. And it will be equally important to keep all color-coded items stored in a systemized fashion.

WELLNESS

Wellness is a conscious and active process of achieving balance and well-being in all areas of your life. As a young professional with ASD, it is imperative that you actively plan for stressors, mitigate the stress when possible, and maintain your holistic wellness to the highest degree possible.

In relation to the impact of stress, three distinct areas of wellness are now highlighted:

NUTRITION

Individuals with ASD often have specific food intolerances, which could result in deficiencies of specific vitamins and minerals. In addition, the intake of sugary food and caffeine often increases as a result of stress. Nutrition is an important aspect of maintaining wellness, so those with ASD need to plan to adjust their eating routine during times of stress, and may need to consider a vitamin regimen.

Eating right can play a part in your ability to manage stress effectively. A balanced diet can positively affect both your physical and mental health. When we are stressed, we tend to eat unhealthily. Some people over-eat or load up on unhealthy types of food, while others eat hardly anything at all. Our bodies require the proper balance of nutrients, many of which are helpful in controlling our bodies' responses to stress. When we load up on sugar or caffeine, our bodies get a temporary boost, but the flash is short-lived, and soon we are right back to where we were. Make sure you continue to eat three balanced meals a day, especially when experiencing increased stress.

SLEEP

Individuals with ASD may also struggle with maintaining a balanced sleep schedule. Whether people get caught up in a favorite video game or simply cannot sleep through the night, this lack of a consistent sleep schedule could heighten the impact of stress. It is vital to maintain a solid and consistent sleep schedule to maintain holistic wellness.

Sleep is as important to our bodies as food. Lack of sleep can affect your emotional state, ability to concentrate, and ability to cope with stress as well as physical health. Research states that an average young adult requires 7–8 hours sleep a night (National Sleep Foundation 2016). Trying to get the right amount of sleep you require is crucial in maintaining a stable emotional and physical state. Staying aware of your physical health by being aware of your diet and sleep habits can help you control the effects of stress on your emotional state.

EXERCISE

Finally, individuals with ASD tend to decline to participate in team sports, exercise classes, or lifting weights in the gym with a lot of other people, but exercise is important to maintain wellness. It can come in the form of individual sports such as running, yoga, or martial arts, among other options. Regardless of which form of physical exercise you do, all are beneficial to maintain a state of wellness during times of stress.

Exercise can be a good stress reliever and can actually increase the chemicals in our bodies that combat depression. Creating an exercise routine does not have to be a lengthy strenuous process. Many gyms offer staff to help you establish a routine that works best for you (Rigler *et al.* 2015a). Stress can create tension in our bodies, and exercise creates an outlet for this tension. It is import for your general well-being to stay active.

Some additional ways to reduce stress are:

- Spend time each night preparing for the next day.

- Get up a few minutes early to give yourself plenty of time to get ready for work.

- Write things down and don't rely on your memory.

- Maintain good communication by checking email and voicemails and taking notes in the process.

- Don't procrastinate.

- Plan ahead.

- Create a contingency plan.

- Have manipulatives at your desk (e.g. stress ball, rubber band).

- Use headphones to drown out distractions or excess noise.

- Take frequent breaks.

- Take a walk outside and get some fresh air.

- Journal your thoughts after each day.

What are some other things you have found that help you reduce stress in your life?

_____

_____

_____

_____

COPING STRATEGIES

Some coping strategies work for some that might not work for others. They can be different for internal versus external stressors. For internal stressors, you could use deep breathing or meditation, for example. For external stressors, you could rely on environmental management and workplace accommodations. Stress management plans and wellness efforts can be helpful for both internal and external stressors.

For most people, one of the first physical indicators of stress is a change in breathing rhythm. When stressed, our breathing becomes shallow and labored, which inhibits the amount of oxygen that gets to the brain, which might result in various symptoms of stress (Rigler *et al.* 2015a), as outlined earlier, in Lesson 1, such as headaches, sleep problems, and general mood disruption. In order to normalize the oxygen levels in the brain, concentrate on regulating your breathing pattern.

One of the quickest and most effective ways to reduce stress is to practice deep breathing techniques. This signals your brain to communicate to your body, which then signals that you're regaining control. To practice, find a quiet location, and practice the following pattern in order:

- Allow yourself to be free of distractions for 5–10 minutes.

- Inhale for ten seconds.

- Hold your breath for a count of ten.

- Exhale for ten seconds.

- Repeat at least ten times.

STRESS MANAGEMENT PLAN

Part of managing stress is being able to identify your triggers, learning how your body reacts, physically and emotionally, and part of the process of taking responsibility for managing your stress is in understanding how others may perceive your reaction, and how you choose to implement your coping strategies. Figuring out what strategies to implement and how to cope with the various situations means creating a stress management plan (see below).

The best time to develop a plan is when little to no stressors are present; if you are not emotionally charged by stress, you will be able to develop a more realistic plan. This way, when stressors are present, you will have determined the best possible approach to coping with stress.

Use the chart below to develop your own stress management plan. An example is given in the first row.

STRESS MANAGEMENT PLAN

Professional stressor	How it feels	How others see it	Coping strategy
Your team gets a bad report back on a project you worked so hard on. You don't understand what went wrong or why others did not pull their weight	Your chest feels tight and your breathing pattern is irregular. You feel like you want to cry and shout at your co-workers	If you cry or shout at your co-workers they may see you as disrespectful and threating. They may ask you to leave and treat you differently in the future	Leave the situation and go for a walk for some fresh air. When you have had time to think, write down some questions or concerns you have about the project. Have someone you trust review your comments before you share them at the next staff meeting

How to Recharge

Experiencing stress is inevitable, and frustrations are a normal part of professional development; managing your emotions while under stress can also be difficult. Doing things that help you stay motivated and interest you outside of work is one way for you to recharge your energy. This can help prevent burnout, meltdowns at work, and even improve your overall work performance. When you think about recharging yourself, compare it to recharging your phone every night. If you forget to plug it in or never charge it, your phone will not perform when you need it to because its battery is drained. As a young professional your "battery" will drain if you do not develop a plan for recharging it.

There are several ways people can recharge, but you must figure out what works best for you and for your needs.

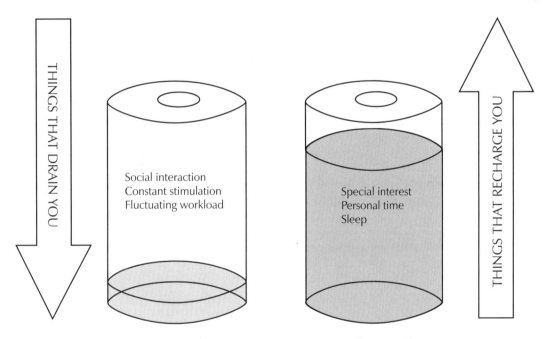

FIGURE 5.2 RECHARGING YOUR "BATTERY"

What drains your "battery"?

_____

_____

_____

What recharges your "battery"?

_____

_____

_____

PERSONAL TIME

Because your job is an environment of interaction, stress can sometimes be reduced by simply limiting social contact to allow for some personal time. This doesn't mean that it would be reasonable to stay in your office for days on end, but there are ways to incorporate "alone time" throughout your day. As a young professional with ASD, you may find that the constant social atmosphere of the workplace is exhausting. Some companies offer a few personal days throughout the year, but most of the time you have to request that day well in advance. Incorporate some personal time into each day, and also recognize when more than an hour or two is needed. Taking some personal time to refocus and re-energize can make a difference in the way your attitude and behavior are expressed while interacting with co-workers, friends and family.

One option might be to find time for personal relationships by scheduling an hour or longer before bed to read, play video games, go for a walk, watch a movie, or learn more about a non-work-related special interest. Be mindful, though, of the time limit you set up for yourself, and make sure that it doesn't become too time-consuming. If managed appropriately, this is a good way to take your mind off work and the social demands of being a young professional. Understanding your limits and taking personal time when needed can potentially make your work performance more effective, helps reduce stress and the potential of a meltdown, and allows you an opportunity to recharge.

Now reflect back on Lesson 1 and consider how you might respond to situations using the strengths you have identified in this lesson.

Situation	Response	Comment
Your alarm didn't go off and now you're running late for work		
Your co-workers leave the coffee station in a mess		
You get called to an impromptu meeting		
The seat you usually sit in during staff meetings is taken by someone else		
Your co-workers have a disagreement about a task outside your office		
In the middle of a meeting your pen runs out of ink		

You have to walk through a crowd of people to get to your desk every morning		
You were asked to collaborate with a different department on a project		
A meeting time is changed to a later date		
Your co-worker likes to play music loudly while they work		
Two co-workers are conferring outside your office or cubical		
You worked really hard on a presentation and now the USB stick is missing from your desk		
Your boss announces a change in the deadline for an upcoming project		
Your friend cancelled plans to go to a movie after work		
Your boss asks you to stay late to finish the project you have been working on		

LESSON 3: RESPONDING TO STRESS IN THE WORKPLACE

Exposing yourself to stress as a new professional is an inevitable part of any job or career path you may take. While some situations or circumstances may provoke more stress than others, the effects of stress do not have to have a long-lasting negative impact on your physical, emotional, or professional well-being. Although as a young adult with ASD you might process the impact of stress differently, it is vital to maintain control and to take responsibility for your responses and to avoid emotionally charged reactions.

Reflect on what you have learned about yourself:

What triggers your stress?

_____

_____

_____

What responses do you have to stress?

_____

_____

_____

What coping strategies work for you, and have you developed a plan to recharge your energy?

_____

_____

_____

It is now time to think about how you might respond to stress in the workplace. Read through the following scenarios, and describe how you might handle the different triggers, stressful situations, and what coping strategies you might have used.

CHAD'S STORY

Chad is 33 years old and enjoys spending time outdoors hiking and relaxing on the lake. He has been working as a manager in a retail store for several years, and enjoys his work. Although the hours are long, he really likes the people he works with. Part of Chad's responsibility includes conducting quarterly inventories and reporting the results to his corporate headquarters. This requires attention to detail, long hours, and collaboration with co-workers. As the deadline for the next inventory approaches, one of Chad's most dependable employees becomes ill and is off from work for several days. His duties are assumed by an employee who has much less experience. Chad discovers the back-up employee has failed to enter several shipments into the store's inventory, and he is forced to work extra hours correcting the mistake. Because of this, he has to cancel a weekend on the lake with friends.

Monday, when the employees report to work, Chad is not himself. He is rude to other employees and spends extended time in his office. Chad is short with customers and even refused to help a vendor with questions. He is so stressed that he is forced to take the afternoon off to regroup.

What symptoms of stress did Chad have?

_____

_____

_____

_____

How did Chad recharge and manage his stress?

_____

_____

_____

_____

What could Chad have done to prevent the stress?

_____

_____

_____

_____

SONYA'S STORY

Sonya is a bank teller who is going back to school to finish her MBA. The bank she works for now requires the tellers to sell products such as credit cards and mortgage loans to their customers. The bank keeps track of her sales, and constantly reminds her of the requirements of the position. When her grade for the last paper for her MBA was posted, it was lower than she expected, and she is now under pressure to get a higher score on the next text or she will fail the class. When she arrived home after work, she discovered that her refrigerator in her apartment had broken and her food had spoiled.

When her roommate came home in a good mood after spending the day shopping and having dinner with friends, Sonya broke down. She began to doubt the worth of finishing her degree, feared she might lose her job if she didn't perform to her employer's expectations, and did not know how she could afford to replace the food that had been spoiled. The next day at work, she was not herself, and was short with the bank's customers.

What might Sonya do to alleviate some stressors in her life?

_____

_____

_____

_____

_____

_____

What could Sonya do to manage the stress of balancing life (school, relationships, and work)?

_____

_____

_____

_____

_____

What might your response have been in this situation?

_____

_____

_____

_____

COURTNEY'S STORY

Courtney is an engineer in an automotive parts factory. The company she works for recently received a contract for a new line of parts, and so the workload has gone up dramatically. In a meeting with other engineers, Courtney was assigned tasks she had never done before with a short timeline for completion. Because of the increase in business, Courtney had been working a lot of overtime and was not getting much rest. When pushed to take on the work, she started to cry and ran from the room. It took her several minutes to pull herself together, but she was embarrassed to re-enter the meeting.

How might Courtney re-enter the meeting appropriately?

_____

_____

_____

_____

_____

What might Courtney do to maintain control of her emotions?

_____

_____

_____

_____

How can Courtney prevent this from happening in the future?

_____

_____

_____

_____

LESSON 4: PROFESSIONAL TOOL FOR MANAGING STRESS

The idea behind creating a wellness plan is to give young professionals the opportunity to be proactive in using a healthy coping strategy. Staying healthy will help you optimize your performance, stay alert, and feel good, but you will also benefit from the habitual routine and structure associated with self-care, living independently, and finding your place in a career (Meeks *et al.* 2016). By being proactive you are investing energy into managing your stress, preventing burnout, and avoiding unhealthy levels of stress that could have a negative impact on you.

A sample wellness plan is provided below that identifies categories or areas to focus your attention on as major objectives. The categories include "Physical and nutritional health," "Leisure time," "Relationships," and "Workplace boundaries." Each of these categories allows you the opportunity to focus on setting up personal goals that will help you manage the stress associated with becoming a professional.

Table 5.1 Wellness plan

Major objective	Personal goals
Physical and nutritional health	1. Maintain exercise regime of 30 minutes per day 2. Get an average of eight hours of sleep each night 3. Take lunch to work three times a week
Leisure time	1. Play one hour of video games twice a week 2. Find one new fun book to read a month 3. Attend club meetings twice a month
Relationships	1. Make time for friends outside of work once a week 2. Check in with family every Sunday night via phone 3. Have lunch with co-workers twice a week
Workplace boundaries	1. Make a conscious effort to respect the privacy of co-workers 2. Limit your response to "water cooler" conversations to three minutes or less 3. Be mindful of the limits of your own personal life

After reviewing this plan, take some time to consider your own well-being. Use the category titled "Other" so you have the opportunity to identify major objectives you have that may differ from the example given above.

⬇ WELLNESS PLAN

Major objective	Personal goals
Physical and nutritional health	1. 2. 3.
Leisure time	1. 2. 3.
Relationships	1. 2. 3.
Workplace boundaries	1. 2. 3.
Other	1. 2. 3.

Creating your own personal wellness plan will help promote workplace satisfaction while promoting your own well-being. Use this professional tool weekly as a way to help hold yourself accountable and to work towards your goal of professionalism. Develop your plan at the beginning of the month, and evaluate its effectiveness each Sunday before beginning your working week.

By using this tool to outline the ways in which you are struggling mentally or physically, you can start to make a specific plan for your needs as an individual, which will help you to become more conscious of the areas that need the most improvement.

BACK TO BASICS

B 1 2 3	**Behavior**	Are you setting boundaries? Are you using your identified coping strategies? Are you being productive? What are you doing to actively manage your emotions?
A 1 2 3	**Academics**	Are you remaining mindful of your triggers? Are you recognizing and using your strengths to control stress? Do you feel in control of your responses to stress?
S 1 2 3	**Self-care**	Are you eating healthily? Are you maintaining appropriate hygiene? Are you sleeping? Are you holding yourself accountable to your wellness plan? Are you making time for self-care activities?
I 1 2 3	**Interaction**	Are you using your support resources and team? Do you feel connected? Are you able to communicate your concerns with others appropriately? Do you feel like you are part of the team?
C 1 2 3	**Community**	Do you feel like you belong? Are you asking for help when needed? Are you working cohesively as a team member? Are your reactions to stress appropriate?
S 1 2 3	**Self-monitoring**	Are you advocating for your needs? Are you implementing a recharging routine? Are you planning time for social activities?

GOALS

Personal:

Aptitude:

Social:

⬇ BACK TO BASICS: RATE YOURSELF

B	**Behavior** 1 2 3	**Comments**
A	**Academics** 1 2 3	**Comments**
S	**Self-care** 1 2 3	**Comments**
I	**Interaction** 1 2 3	**Comments**
C	**Community** 1 2 3	**Comments**
S	**Self-monitoring** 1 2 3	**Comments**

GOALS

Personal:

Aptitude:

Social:

Chapter 6

COLLABORATION AND TEAMWORK

INTRODUCTION

The workplace is an interesting, confusing, and incredibly social setting that can be difficult to navigate but fulfilling when the path is clear. Whether the workplace is an engineering lab, a law firm, a restaurant, or an accounting office, there will be some level of collaboration expected. There are very few career options in which an individual will work alone with no involvement from others to complete a task. The idea of teamwork and collaboration may be a topic that causes frustration for people with ASD, but it is something that should be managed rather than avoided.

Teamwork may cause frustration for many reasons, but the three most commonly discussed sources of frustration are high expectations of work output, social communication confusion, and lack of confidence in other team members (Rigler *et al.* 2015b).

People with ASD tend to have very high expectations for themselves and of the work they produce, but those around them may not share this level of expectation. Throughout the educational experience, most likely collaborative work was the expectation, but this experience was often not favorable for many students with ASD. This carried-over negative perception of teamwork could skew how you view professional teamwork in the workplace.

Social communication confusion is another reason why working in groups can be highly stressful for those with ASD. Not only do individuals have to share a common goal, manage the expectations, monitor task progress and completion, communicate about the progress, and share control over the work at hand, but they also must prepare for social interaction and practice communication to avoid any social miscues that could potentially occur. This added stressor often contributes to professionals with ASD feeling overwhelmed. The energy required to manage the social aspect of teamwork is tremendous and could easily detract from the final product, or cause the outcome to be less optimal than expected (Rigler *et al.* 2015b).

Finally, people with ASD tend to avoid working collaboratively because they are not confident that other group members will or can contribute the same level of cognitive energy and commitment to the project. This fear could also come from the mismanagement of collaborative work throughout school, which carries over into the workplace. While this concern may have been valid in school, there is a definitive shift when individuals enter the workforce. When a person's livelihood is on the line, and competition for positive performance evaluations and pay rises replace competition for grades, the expectation of the competency of professional partners increases.

Regardless of what formed the perception of teamwork for a person with ASD, it is imperative that this view be challenged. The probability of entering a career with little expectation of teamwork and collaboration is low, so it is in your best interests to examine the difficulties and biases against teamwork, and to develop a plan for how this expectation can be managed effectively.

The first step in developing this plan is to understand the purpose of professional teamwork.

LESSON 1: THE PURPOSE OF TEAMWORK

The importance of being able to participate in and contribute to a team in the workplace has been established, but people with ASD may misunderstand the purpose behind teamwork. As with many things, developing a strong understanding of why teamwork is important can help professionals with ASD embrace this important aspect of a career. Rather than viewing the aspect of collaborating and creating professional work teams as shallow business initiatives that have no true benefit, those with ASD can begin to see the genuine benefit of working in a productive team. Once purpose is established, workers can then spend time developing solid collaborative work skills to make the most of teamwork.

The purpose of teamwork is outlined as follows, taken from the Management Study Guide (2015):

- businesses are task-focused and project completion is of top priority

- project sustainability

- project completion is done at a faster pace

- competition among team members creates a better end result

- team members all have something to contribute and a role to fill.

As professionals enter the workforce, the shift to become task-oriented becomes very clear. The focus on the completion of projects can occasionally cause distress for people with ASD due to the need to produce a perfect product. The high expectations people with ASD put on themselves is often seen as a true strength, but can also be limiting when it comes to project completion. It could, in fact, be viewed as a major obstacle in maintaining employment for those with ASD. The ability to plan a project, manage work effort and time commitments, and the completion of the project are basic requirements of many jobs (Bissonnette 2013). By approaching work collaboratively, team members can help each other maintain a high level of expectations along with the expected project completion rate, and avoid the difficulties of getting stuck in the process.

Within the workplace it is also very important for more than one individual to have an understanding of the ongoing work as it is being completed. At any time, something could happen and someone may become ill, have a family emergency, lose a job, etc., so for a project or task to be sustained, it is imperative for more than one individual to have an understanding of where the work is in process. While many with ASD like to keep projects to themselves until they are completed them to their high levels of personal expectation, this could cause a significantly negative impact on the completion of the work if something should happen and that individual is no longer able to work on the project. In this case, the team would most likely have to start from the very beginning, and all the high quality work would be lost. By approaching work collaboratively, team members can stay apprised of the stages of completion and the work that is still needed, and project completion can stay on track regardless of the changing of any team members.

Project completion in a timely manner is an expectation of all jobs. There is an expectation that work will be completed to a high standard and on time, which can be an obstacle to employment for people with ASD. A considerable skill set difficulty for people with ASD is lack of executive function. Executive function skills include task initiation, action planning and organization, effort maintenance, emotional regulation, sustaining focus, and working memory (Rigler *et al.* 2015a). A breakdown in any one of these processes could cause an individual to get stuck and not be able to complete a project on time. Working collaboratively on a team could allow for other team members to recognize when a colleague has become stuck, and remind them of the deadline for completion, assisting with the necessary steps to encourage that completion at a faster pace.

A healthy level of competition is a good idea in most realms, including the workplace. The competition to be recognized for good work, receiving a positive performance evaluation, or being awarded an honor for a project is a good way to receive a raise and a promotion, so competition in work is always present. Professionals with ASD tend to focus heavily on individual work, and don't put much emphasis on the work of others. While the expectation individuals with ASD put on themselves tends to be higher than their peers, without an understanding of the level of competence of those peers, they may inadvertently take themselves out of consideration for the professional accolades. While the high standard of work is a great quality to maintain, without developing an understanding of what others are accomplishing, those with ASD will likely not be able to gauge their own work accomplishments. By approaching work collaboratively, team members with ASD can maintain a constant understanding of the proficiency of their co-workers, and adjust their own effort accordingly, to keep themselves in the competition for career advancement.

It is also important for those with ASD to understand that every person in the work environment has something to contribute and something to gain. Every person has significant strengths as well as weaknesses, and every person has a role to fill. Consider the idea of teams in relation to a sports team. A football team can only be good if each position is represented equally. If a team has a strong quarterback, but no receiver, the team will never have completed pass plays. The same can be said for a work group. If the group has several people who initiate tasks but no thinkers, they will start on the project quickly, but may not be working towards the same goal (Rigler *et al.* 2015c). Initiators put the group in motion while thinkers provide direction and are consistently aware of the important details.

Individuals with ASD have high expectations not only of themselves, but also of others with whom they work. If these expectations are realistic, this could contribute to great team success. If the expectations are unrealistic, this could turn other group members off, and the individual with ASD may be isolated from the group. In a collaborative team, if everyone is recognized for what they have to offer to the group and roles are developed, they will experience considerable and sustained success together.

LESSON 2: INDIVIDUAL CONTRIBUTIONS

Every person in a work team has individualized strengths that got them hired for the job they hold. Some people are very good at networking and connecting people and ideas, while others are very good at analyzing and categorizing information into a logical order. Some team members are very technologically sound while others are better at interpersonal interactions. Regardless of the strengths and skills a person brings to the team, they should all be recognized and appreciated.

Personally, people with ASD tend to value relationships characterized by loyalty and dependability, engage in authentic conversations free of hidden meanings or an agenda, seek sincere and genuine relationships, and they tend to accept people at "face value." They also have the ability to listen while suspending judgment of others, they seek substantial relationships while appreciating the contributions of others, avoiding trivial "small talk," they tend to have clear values unaffected by political/social pressures, and are often the "social unsung heroes," with trusting optimism, which means that they are often the frequent victims of the social weaknesses of others (Attwood 1999). While these personal strengths may not be evident in all people with ASD, they have been observed in many people with ASD.

Professionally, those with ASD have a different but equally valuable set of strengths. The National Autism Society discusses these strengths in their guide for employing people with autism (2012). Although the list is not all-inclusive, the following are some of the most recognized work-related strengths associated with ASD:

- **Attention to detail:** Professionals with ASD tend to be acutely aware of details that are often overlooked by others. This supports the notion that people with ASD can recognize patterns and identify problems in a system before others.

- **Creative problem solving:** Professionals with ASD tend to prefer thinking in structured and logical ways. This, coupled with the ability to recognize fine details, allows people with ASD to be efficient and innovative when solving problems.

- **High levels of concentration:** Professionals with ASD often enjoy focusing on details and doing repetitive work that others may find monotonous. Along with the commitment to completion, this level of concentration allows people with ASD to work for hours without being distracted by what is going on around them.

- **Reliability:** Professionals with ASD tend to be very ethical and committed to their work. This often results in a dependable, loyal, honest worker operating with great integrity. People with ASD demonstrate high levels of punctuality and attendance.

- **Technical ability:** Professionals with ASD often have elevated technical skills that are considered valuable in the majority of work opportunities. This, in partnership with their creative problem-solving skills, makes people with ASD valuable additions to many workplaces.

- **Specialized interests:** As a component of ASD, they will often have highly specialized and focused interests. If these interests are connected to the work at hand, professionals with ASD will often develop detailed factual knowledge about that area, and will research to stay up-to-date on those facts. This allows those with ASD to be highly knowledgeable workers who can teach others the information they understand so clearly.

- **Excellent memory:** It is reported that people with ASD have a strong memory (Ozonoff, Dawson and McPartland 2015), which makes them consistent and dependable workers. This allows professionals with ASD to develop and remember routines that contribute to reliable workplace structures.

- **Rule-following capabilities:** Professionals with ASD tend to be strict rule followers in both their personal and professional lives. If they define something as a rule, they will likely follow that rule consistently. This strength creates highly ethical and honest workers.

- **Retention:** People with ASD often have a need to develop and maintain a routine. Once this routine is established, a professional with ASD will be content to stick with the routine for a long period of time. This means that once people with ASD are settled into the routine of their job, they will likely stay in that role considerably longer than colleagues without ASD.

- **Resourceful:** People with ASD have often developed strategies and tools to overcome difficulties throughout their lives, and have become extremely resourceful and resilient. This strength, combined with a need to complete tasks, can result in strong workers who will not give up when things become difficult. Instead, they will more likely develop a strategic and creative solution to the problem.

It is important to recognize that not all people with ASD will possess these strengths equally, but because they are related to ASD, it is likely that they will possess some of them. It is also important to recognize that because these strengths are related to ASD, if you do not currently relate to one of them, it is likely that you can work to develop them as a professional strength.

Look at the following chart as an example of how to graph your interpretations of your own strengths, and then fill in your own. Please confer with those close to you to evaluate your responses and receive feedback about their interpretation.

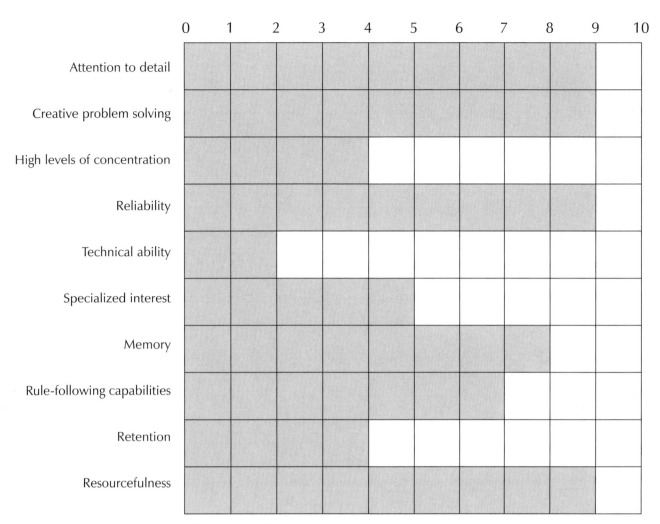

FIGURE 6.1 EXAMPLE OF A TOP TEN STRENGTHS CHART

	0	1	2	3	4	5	6	7	8	9	10
Attention to detail											
Creative problem solving											
High levels of concentration											
Reliability											
Technical ability											
Specialized interest											
Memory											
Rule-following capabilities											
Retention											
Resourcefulness											

LESSON 3: CONFLICT RESOLUTION

Collaborative teamwork is an important aspect of a successful work experience, but can also contribute to workplace conflict. Successful teams focus not only on the completion of a project, but also on recognizing team members' strengths, communicating effectively, negotiating so everyone feels valued, and reaching the goal together. With so many opportunities for social miscues, conflict is a real possibility, but the fear of that conflict should not be a reason to avoid working collaboratively.

Use the following scenarios regarding conflict resolution in the workplace to begin developing your own conflict resolution skills. Evaluate how the people in the scenarios managed conflict, and use their experiences to guide your professional needs analysis and skills development.

CHARLES' STORY

Charles is a recent graduate with an IT degree from a highly respected university. He was always at the top of his class, and graduated with a 3.9 GPA, so he came in to the job feeling very competent and confident in his skills. After working successfully on the job for two months, he was included in a large-scale website design project. This project is potentially very lucrative for his company if the team produces the quality of work expected by the client. This is the first time Charles has been expected to work on a collaborative team, and he is very nervous about it. Because he is so competent in design, he is concerned that the other members of the team will not be able to keep up with him on the project, and that their incompetence will make him look bad to the boss.

During the first meeting, Charles sits quietly while the other team members are talking about ideas for the project. They are excited to be working together, and spend time talking about personal things to get to know each other, as well as discussing the project at hand. After 45 minutes of listening to the rambling conversations, Charles stands up and leaves the room.

The next week, the group meets again to get started on the project, but Charles already has a well-outlined plan in place. He goes to the meeting with a detailed agenda, with copies of his design plan for all the team members, and is feeling confident that the others will like his plan. He joins the group and begins to hand out his plan to each member and says, "After we wasted so much time at the last meeting, I decided to come up with an agenda and a plan for the project and have outlined it in this document. I assigned everyone a task to work on so we can meet the expected deadline."

Another team member steps in and says he has an idea for the design project as well. He begins to share his idea with the group, and Charles can tell that the plan is not as well developed as his, and he questions the capability of the team member. However, the other team members are actively discussing the other plan as a possibility instead of his. Charles then stands up and tells the group, "This plan is subpar and I won't be a part of a group that does subpar work," and walks out of the meeting angrily.

What could happen as a result of Charles' actions?

_____

_____

_____

_____

How could Charles have more effectively communicated his thoughts?

_____

_____

_____

_____

How can Charles repair the damage he has done to the team, and complete the project effectively?

_____

_____

_____

_____

MOLLY'S STORY

Molly is in her first job as a graphics artist and is concerned about an upcoming project in which four of her colleagues will be working together to create a marketing tool for a new company in town. This is a project she is very excited about because the client is a new horse ranch in town that is offering equine therapy for people with disabilities. Molly loves horses and has studied all she can about them; she is also a strong advocate for disability rights, so this project combines her interests perfectly. Molly has many ideas for capturing what the ranch can do for the community, and can't wait to share them with the group.

Molly arrives to the first meeting with the group, and notices that everyone is already talking like they know each other, and she feels awkward joining in, so she just sits quietly while everyone continues on with their conversations. At some point, the conversations shift to talking about the project, but Molly misses the transition and now the group is talking about an idea that someone has brought up. Molly's idea is completely different, so she questions whether she misunderstood the project and decides not to share her idea.

Molly sits quietly through the entire meeting, taking mental notes of ideas, and begins processing the information. At one point, a team member tells Molly that her task on the project is to think about the color scheme of the branding for the company, but she is not excited about this task. Because Molly loves horses so much, she is against the use of branding irons on horses, and she questions why it would matter what color the branding iron is anyway.

Regardless of her feelings about the subject, Molly works on her portion of the project and brings some color schemes and design ideas for the branding iron to the next meeting. As she stands to present her ideas about the branding iron, the group begins to laugh together and the person who assigned the tasks says, "Seriously? I was talking about the branding for the company so we can develop marketing materials, not a branding iron." Molly quickly leaves the room so the other team members can't see her cry.

How could Molly have created an opportunity for herself to share her idea for the project?

_____

_____

_____

_____

What possibly contributed to Molly's confusion about her assigned task?

_____

_____

_____

_____

Molly has to work with this team in the future, so how can she address this situation and help the team understand that she is a competent team member?

_____

_____

_____

_____

JUSTIN'S STORY

Justin works as a computer engineer at a large global company. One of his roles is to investigate potential programming difficulties and to develop solutions for those difficulties. His current project is to work with a group of colleagues to fix a software bug in a program that is integral to company operations. This software has been used for many years, and was internally developed by an engineer to help make the company's processes more effective.

Over the course of his employment at this company, Justin has discovered that there are many processes that have been put into place and that have been maintained out of habit, but there are other avenues for completing processes more efficiently, if the group is willing to make a few changes. Because Justin can recognize the details that the rest of the group overlooks and can recognize patterns fluidly, he has discovered a more intuitive path to accomplish the same process the original software was designed to do in fewer steps. And it would take significantly more time to try to fix the problem rather than develop a new software package.

Justin brought this idea to the work group as a potential solution to the problem and said, "This old software was developed years ago by some old engineer who was clearly out of the field for quite some time. The software has been outdated for a long time and I can't believe this company is still trying to use such an archaic software package. I can develop a better and more intuitive program in less time than what it would take to fix all the problems with this current software. We don't have to continue to use some outdated software just because some old guy that this company liked developed it. It is time to move into this century."

Justin's comments were received with silence and blank looks, when one of the team members stood up and said, "That old engineer that developed this archaic system was my grandfather," then left the room. Everyone on the team was quiet and staring at Justin, who didn't know what to say.

How was Justin's comment offensive to his teammate?

_____

_____

_____

_____

What can Justin say to the teammate to repair the relationship?

_____

_____

_____

_____

How could Justin have pitched his idea to the team in a more effective way?

_____

_____

_____

_____

MELISSA'S STORY

Melissa is a senior in college and has been a strong advocate for educating others about ASD. She is a Psychology major and looks forward to a future of advocacy and outreach to help other young girls in the community realize their full potential in relation to their ASD diagnosis. Melissa was diagnosed as a teen, and the diagnosis explained a lot for her, and was actually a relief for her. She used to have frequent meltdowns in which she would cry hysterically and wring her hands quickly until she was able to control her environment. However, since coming to college, her meltdowns decreased significantly.

During her junior year of college, Melissa was helping with a retreat intended for college students with ASD. She has long been seen as a leader and mentor for others, so this role was an expected next step for her. She helps to plan community activities and outreach for young women in the community with ASD, and has taken on leadership roles and speaking opportunities for well over a year, and had not had any meltdowns with the added pressure.

During the dinner portion of the retreat, Melissa went to the buffet to get her food and when she returned, someone was sitting in her seat and had moved her backpack. Melissa felt the familiar feeling of an upcoming meltdown, but knew that if she exhibited her typical meltdown behaviors in front of everyone, she would not be seen in the same way. She set her plate down and removed herself from the dining room. She went to the bathroom, locked the door, and cried into a wad of toilet paper as quietly as she could. When she felt the meltdown had run its course, Melissa came out of the stall and washed her face with cool water. She waited a few minutes until her face was no longer red and tear-stained, and then rejoined the group.

Melissa approached the person who had moved her bag and sat in her seat and simply stated, "I had my bag sitting here to save my seat and when my plan gets disrupted, it makes me very anxious. In the future, please do not move my things because that is a sign that I plan to sit there."

The person who sat in her seat immediately responded with, "I'm so sorry, I had no idea. Let me move over so you can have your seat. Thanks for letting me know."

How might others have viewed Melissa if she had yelled and cried in front of everyone?

_____

_____

_____

_____

What is a different way Melissa could have managed this situation?

_____

_____

_____

_____

As a leader, it is important for Melissa to maintain composure until she finds the right place and right time to safely let her meltdown happen. Where and when is a good time to let these feeling out in the workplace?

_____

_____

_____

_____

How have you managed meltdowns in the past to avoid damaging relationships?

_____

_____

_____

_____

LESSON 4: PROFESSIONAL TOOL FOR DEFINING YOUR ROLE IN A TEAM

There is a component to being successful in the work setting that involves being able to use your skills and knowledge in the way you prefer that not only allows you to be successful in your career, but also allows you to be comfortable and happy in doing so. These preferences can help you outline your roles in any collaborative team. This tool was originally developed for the college setting, and has been modified to be used in the professional setting from Rigler *et al.* (2015c).

Read the following pairs of statements, and tick which statement most closely matches your preference in regards to working on a collaborative team, then total the number of ticks in each column.

Plan	Do
☐ I like to set timelines	☐ I work best under pressure
☐ I work best with a plan in place	☐ I like to just start the project
☐ I like to set goals	☐ The goal is to get the project finished
☐ I'm good at developing a vision	☐ I can follow a plan well
☐ I like to organize projects	☐ It is better for people to assign me tasks
☐ It is best to assign roles to team members	☐ Everyone contributes in their own way
☐ I use a good planning system	☐ I have a good memory
☐ I need to set guidelines for projects	☐ I like to be creative
☐ Measurable outcomes are important	☐ Task completion is what is important
☐ I like to clarify expectations in the beginning	☐ I like to just get to work
Total:	Total:

The information gathered through this activity allows you to examine your preference between being a person who likes to "plan" or a person who likes to "do" on a team project. The total number gives you an indication for whether you like to take part in creating the timeline for a project and defining the success indicators, or if you would prefer to get started on the project right away.

A person who likes to "plan" tends to think about the details of the project while projecting a potential timeline for completion and roles for each member. A person who prefers to work in this way tends to rather have guidelines and group norms outlined to alleviate any potential for conflict in the future. This person also values the process rather than the completed product.

A person who likes to "do" is action-oriented and would prefer to get to work right away. A person with this preference may feel that planning the project is a waste of time, and would rather just start working. The goal of a person who likes to "do" is often to complete the project as efficiently as possible. This person values the end product rather than the process of the group.

Both perspectives are important in the operations of a collaborative team group and each team must have people who prefer to "plan" and "do" to successfully complete the assigned task. If a group lacks a plan, the project will have no direction; conversely, if a project lacks action, the project will be have a great plan for success, but may never achieve completion.

Now take some time to analyze the next set of statements and decide which one most reflects your preference as part of a work group. Remember that each statement is valid and necessary for the effective completion of every collaborative project. Base your answers on your personal preference in collaborative projects.

Lead	Connect
☐ I like to look for people's strengths	☐ I can identify commonalities
☐ I like to direct the process	☐ I like to partner throughout the process
☐ It is very important to monitor progress	☐ It is important to monitor communication
☐ I like to assign tasks to different members	☐ I like to watch roles evolve
☐ I feel better when I define the goals	☐ I enjoy developing the goals as a team
☐ I enjoy taking risks to be innovative	☐ Innovation occurs through partnerships
☐ I can communicate the objectives clearly	☐ I can identify progress from each member
☐ I am confident in my ability	☐ I am confident in the ability of my team
☐ I value the perspective of each member	☐ I value the linkages between each member
☐ I can keep the team motivated to the end	☐ I can help build lasting partnerships
Total:	Total:

The total number in each column indicates whether you prefer to "lead" the team members to effectively and efficiently complete the project, or whether you prefer to "connect" the interests, talents, and skills of group members to develop strong partnerships for the betterment of the group.

A person who likes to "lead" a group project tends to be confident in their own competency and ability to inspire the other group members to work towards the same goal. A person who likes to "lead" values the ability to inspire and guide, and may view success in terms of the individual development and growth of each team member.

A person who prefers to "connect" others within a work group tends to observe the strengths and challenges of each person within the group. This person is able to take note of potential connections before becoming actively involved in the process. This observer often recognizes similarities and differences, and helps partnerships within the team develop. A person who likes to "connect" values the relationships between team members, and embraces the idea that a team is more than several individuals working towards the goal; rather, a team is a set of individuals with complementary talents and strengths.

You should now have an indication of your preference in each of these areas. Take some time to document the total number for each set below. Use this information for the next step to compete this tool.

Plan_____	Do_____
Lead_____	Connect_____

To identify your optimal role within a work team, mark the identified numbers on the corresponding x and y-axis on the following chart. On each line identify two points and mark them with a circle. Within each quadrant, mark the coordinate points with a star. Draw a solid line connecting each star to form a rectangle in the corresponding area of the graph. Make sure your lines also intersect with the coordinating circles. This will help you identify your top two roles and the harmonizing roles you should seek out in others. Use the following example as a guide for this activity.

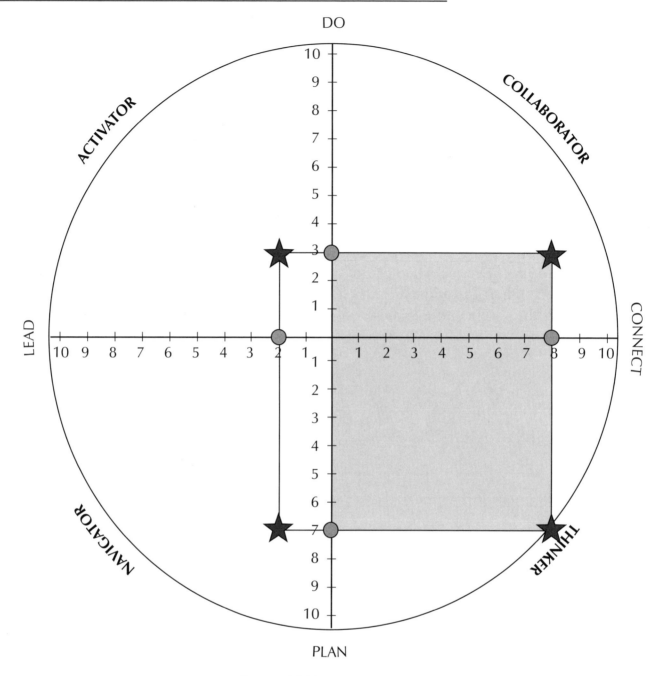

FIGURE 6.2 EXAMPLE OF A ROLE GRAPH

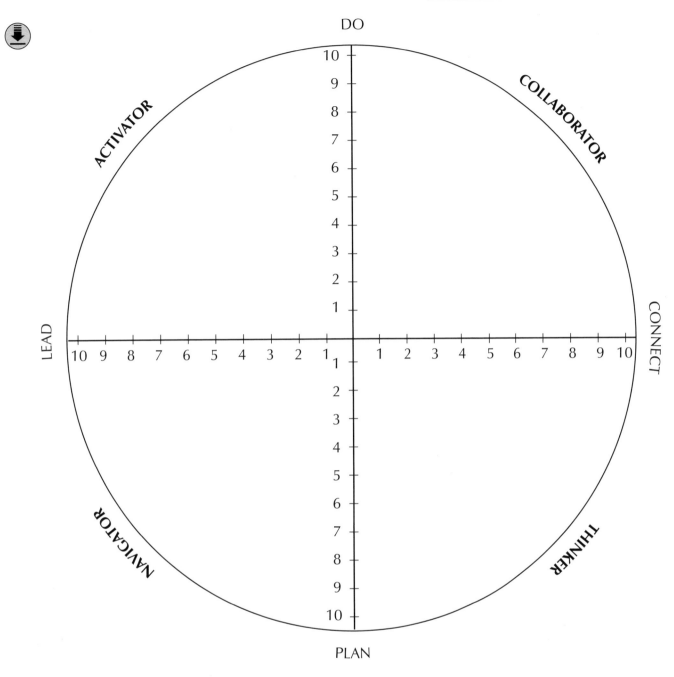

FIGURE 6.3 ROLE PREFERENCE GRAPH

Identify the quadrants where most of your rectangle lies. This is your primary preference for your role in a work group project. This doesn't mean that this is your only preference or the only role you will play in work groups, but this may be where you are the most comfortable. The quadrant where the smallest amount of your rectangle area lies is your least preferable role in a group project. While this is the role you don't choose to take, it is very important to recognize its benefits. This will be your harmonizing role on a team, and the person who fills this role will complement your role in the group. If your star falls outside of the graph area, this is an indication that you only function within one role, and you should focus your attention on the development of another support role as well.

The roles can be described as follows:

Activator: This person initiates the work and starts the group on the right path. This person often takes the ideas of the group members and starts the motion of completion. The activator turns discussions into action and keeps the work moving at a steady pace. The activator will often suggest or assign roles for team members and will outline objectives and timelines for work completion. Throughout the process, the person in this role will remind the team of deadlines and the projected completion date. The primary motive of this person is action. The harmonizing role for the activator is the thinker.

Thinker: This person analyzes all the information presented before making any kind of decision. This person often moves slowly but will be the person who develops a solid plan based on the best interests of the group. The thinker requires all the details of the project and will often spend time discussing these details in depth before attempting to move forward on the plan. The thinker will ensure that the work of the group is staying within the designated plan and timelines while staying focused on the objective of the assignment. The primary motive of the thinker is to analyze details. The harmonizing role for the thinker is the activator.

Navigator: This person directs the work of the team from the beginning to completion. This person may naturally take the lead on projects and set the plan in place. After the project is underway, this person may back out and guide the project from behind the scenes while encouraging other members. The navigator has a dynamic personality and is trusted and provides direction while steering the group through the process. The person who takes this role does not necessarily have positional leadership, but has the potential to guide the team. The primary motive of the navigator is to provide direction. The harmonizing role for the navigator is the collaborator.

Collaborator: This person makes connections between the other members. This person encourages communication and idea sharing while giving encouragement to all the other team members. The collaborator ensures that all members are involved and active in the project as they recognize and validate each person's strengths. The person in this role is typically likable and can effectively encourage the cohesion of the team. The primary motive of the collaborator is to connect team members. The harmonizing role for the collaborator is the navigator.

Identify your primary preference and harmonizing role below. This information can be helpful as you enter collaborative teamwork.

Primary preference:

_____

_____

_____

_____

Harmonizing role:

_____

_____

_____

_____

Working as a member of a team takes a significant amount of cognitive and social energy for professionals with ASD, but this time on work groups will help morale and the development of a sense of belonging with your work group. In addition, working alongside others who think differently than you can help create a better end product. Use this tool to identify not only your own strengths, but also the strengths evident in your co-workers.

BACK TO BASICS

B 1 2 3	**Behavior**	Are you using your strengths and skills set daily at work? Can you identify specifics in your skills set? Are you exploring new ways to use your strengths? Are you practicing flexibility of thought?
A 1 2 3	**Academics**	Are you actively engaging in opportunities to help you identify your professional niche? Do you consider how you contribute to the team? Do you feel balanced in your personal and professional roles?
S 1 2 3	**Self-care**	Are you taking care of your needs? Are you sleeping? Are you able to monitor your stress? Are you maintaining appropriate hygiene? How are you planning for self-care activities?
I 1 2 3	**Interaction**	Are you able to communicate your strengths to others appropriately? Is your harmonizing role creating a balance? Do you notice how others respond to you?
C 1 2 3	**Community**	What are some areas in which you need to feel supported? How do you collaborate with others to further develop your skills and talents? What do others say about your talents? Are you willing to see the contributions others make to a team?
S 1 2 3	**Self-monitoring**	Are you considering how others are contributing their skills? Are you making connections with others? Are you making an effort to engage with others on your team?

GOALS

Personal:

Aptitude:

Social:

⬇ BACK TO BASICS: RATE YOURSELF

B	**Behavior** 1 2 3	Comments
A	**Academics** 1 2 3	Comments
S	**Self-care** 1 2 3	Comments
I	**Interaction** 1 2 3	Comments
C	**Community** 1 2 3	Comments
S	**Self-monitoring** 1 2 3	Comments

GOALS

Personal:

Aptitude:

Social:

Chapter 7

WATER COOLER CULTURE

INTRODUCTION

Many behaviors and social expectations combine to form what we refer to as the "water cooler culture" of companies. Rules within this culture focus less on the professional capacity of individuals to be able to complete their assigned tasks, and more on the ability of an individual to understand and follow a set of unwritten social rules. These could include informal social gatherings on Friday evenings, specific lunch gatherings every Wednesday, or gossip about the weekend around the water cooler. None of these interactions depend on professional ability to get work accomplished, but they do make an impact on whether an individual is perceived as a member of the team. Not participating or making social mistakes during these informal social interactions could ostracize a person, and make them feel disengaged from the team. The first step in taking control of this difficult aspect of professional life is to develop an awareness of the many places where such confusion could happen.

For individuals to successfully navigate the world around them, they must not only be able to use language appropriately, but also understand the social language of those around them (Murza and Nye 2013). Pragmatic language combines all the necessary skills to be able to navigate social language appropriately. It includes skills such as staying on topic, understanding body language and other non-verbal cues, making inferences about other people's perspectives, and sharing conversations appropriately. This skill is difficult for professionals with ASD, and when this skill deficit is combined with the hidden social rules of a workplace culture, maintaining successful employment can be problematic.

In an article written by Holwerda *et al.* (2012), they point out that the difficulties with social skills and communication are typical reasons for employment difficulties, reporting an employment rate of only 25 percent of those who identify as having ASD. The demonstration of social competence and positive social skills is critical to success and independence (see Schall, Wehman and McDonough 2012). While this may be a difficult task for professionals with ASD, with the proper planning and tools, they may have a better opportunity for professional success.

LESSON 1: THE HIDDEN RULES

"Dress down Friday," "Friday afternoon club," and various holiday gatherings are rarely discussed, but strongly infiltrated nuances among company cultures. While many employees may discuss these practices with indifference or disdain (Richards 2015), the majority of the workforce will comply with these activities as they are viewed as non-optional ways for employees to show their commitment to their participation as a work team member and also in the community. These informal rules, as benign as they may seem, are the very obstacles that could interfere with sustained employment for professionals with ASD. The primary objective for those with ASD is to focus on the main duties of the job and completing the work to a high level of success. These informal practices could take away from the focus on work, and encourage individuals to focus more energy on navigating another set of social rules. This could, in return, diminish their work output. The first step in developing tools to navigate the work environment is to understand what these unwritten social rules of the work environment are, and what purpose they serve.

SMALL TALK IN THE WORKPLACE

Small talk in the workplace can sometimes be referred to as "water cooler conversations," not because they happen around the water cooler, but because these brief conversations happen between co-workers as they take a short break. This small amount of chit-chat between colleagues can serve as an avenue for co-workers to build alliances and to develop friendships. While small talk is not something people with ASD tend to engage in, it is inevitable that this is something adults will encounter when they enter the workforce.

The purpose of effectively engaging in such conversations is to build shared experiences with co-workers. Talking about topics that are unrelated to work can help people discover shared interests and hobbies, common backgrounds, and most importantly, can help peers build relationships that are necessary in the development of workplace teams. Topics of these conversations that could help build those relationships may include such things as a recent book you have read, a vacation you took, a series on television you watch, or a video game you may enjoy. This could also be a time to tell a joke, talk about the weather, talk about personal goals, or begin a shared project based on your interests.

If not navigated appropriately, however, such conversations could have a negative impact on morale, and damage those very relationships you are trying to build. There are many topics of conversation that you should avoid completely in the workplace, and the most volatile include, but are not limited to, politics, religion, sex, finances, and personal/medical problems. It may be acceptable to discuss these topics with friends during personal time, but these topics should not be discussed at any time at work.

Keep in mind that these conversations are brief ways to engage with co-workers. These interactions may be a way to identify common interests with colleagues, and could be an avenue to develop a friendship, but in the workplace, they should be limited to five minutes. People with ASD can occasionally lose track of time when discussing a topic that is particularly interesting, so these brief conversations could easily turn into 15-minute monologues. Check your watch or a clock at the beginning of the interaction and limit yourself to five minutes, then return to work. If not monitored, these conversations could detract from the work at hand, and if the conversation is not shared appropriately, the colleague could disengage instead of becoming a stronger partner.

Finally, it is possible for these conversations to become a time to gossip about other co-workers. This could also damage morale and make individuals appear callous and untrustworthy. A good indication that the conversation is turning into gossip is when a sentence begins with "Did you hear…" or "Can you believe that…" Some conversations can be about a colleague and may be positive, but gossip typically focuses on sharing negative things about another person. Rather than trying to decipher if a conversation is positive or turning into negative gossip, develop an exit strategy that does not offend others. This could be as simple as glancing at your phone and saying, "Excuse me, I have to take this call," or it could be based on a social script that you have developed and practiced. An example of such a script that can be used as an exit strategy is as follows:

> "I have to get back to work now, I'm behind on a project that is due today."

Or if you choose to address the gossip directly, the following example of a social script will inform others that you do not engage in gossip, as you do not want to be disrespectful to the other person.

> "I have made a commitment to not discuss others in my conversations. I feel like people should be able to choose what personal information they share."

Decide on the best option and write your social script to use as your exit strategy:

_____

_____

_____

_____

_____

_____

Tips for water cooler conversations:

- Avoid volatile topics.

- Limit interactions to five minutes.

- Avoid gossip.

- Develop an exit strategy.

PEER-TO-PEER INTERACTIONS

Interactions between co-workers can be the most difficult part of the job for a professional with ASD. These tend to be informal and have very few defined rules that have been discussed and agreed on. Neurotypical professionals intuitively understand the social nuances of these types of interactions, but professionals with ASD may have some difficulties with these relationships, which could negatively impact work relationships. Although these interactions could appear friendly and casual, they are still taking place in the work setting, so should carry a professional tone.

The purpose of maintaining a professional tone in all interactions with colleagues is to primarily maintain good personal boundaries on the job. People spend approximately eight hours a day, five days a week, at work with the same individuals. If work relationships are uncomfortable, it could have a negative effect on the whole work team. Any interaction, regardless of how minor, could have a significant impact, so it is vital that all interactions are appropriate. Because it is not as easy to pick up on the social nuances that guide how interactions should proceed, it is best to maintain a high level of professionalism with all colleagues.

People in the workplace have different ways they would like to be addressed, different levels of expectations for conversations, different levels of acceptance for topics of conversations, different levels of comfort with personal boundaries, etc. Refer to the five professional status levels discussed in Chapter 4—these give structure to expectations when they aren't understood intuitively. Professionals with ASD often struggle with developing meaning from context (Kopelson 2015), so it is important to develop and maintain solid and consistent boundaries that are adhered to in all social interactions.

Communication can happen face-to-face, via text messages, on social media, or via email, and they all have varied and unspoken rules that should be adhered to. Because these social rules are unspoken, this may cause confusion and difficulties in the workplace. A common shared difficulty among many individuals with ASD is social communication (van Lange 2015), and this difficulty can have a particularly negative impact on sustained employment. A social faux pas often causes damage to a relationship, but in the workplace, it could result in being fired from a job.

Through face-to-face communication, it is important to recognize that your response and tone can influence a relationship. Individuals with ASD can be blunt and direct in their conversations, which can be perceived as rude or off-putting by others. While this may not be the intention, is it the perception of others that can be defeating. Understanding how others perceive your message will help you understand how others respond to you. It is not the expectation that a professional with ASD must change to fit in at the workplace, but it is advisable to help co-workers develop an understanding of your specific communication style.

Communication through text messages is becoming a more common avenue for conversations. Colleagues don't have to be face-to-face to discuss something, and the conversation can be quick and to the point. The difficulty that could arise through this method of communication, however, is misinterpretation of the message. Occasionally, emotions that are not intended can be read into a text message. For example, if a person types a message all in capital letters, an emotion of anger could be tied to the message, or if a person responds with a very succinct response, the recipient could interpret that the sender is irritated or frustrated. And if a person does not want to communicate with a co-worker, he or she may simply not respond to the text. A neurotypical professional would most likely pick up on this cue and have no further communication with the co-worker, but a professional with ASD could become confused by this lack of response and continue sending text messages to attempt to clarify the interaction. This continued line of text messages could be viewed as harassment and cause significant damage to workplace relationships.

Social media is another way that information is shared in the workplace. Announcements about holiday events, upcoming meetings, or important dates to remember are often communicated this way. It is vital to remember that what you put on social media can be viewed by anyone, including your current or potential future boss. Regardless of the social media applications you choose to use, the method of using these sites must shift when you enter the workforce. These sites can be highly effective in marketing your work and yourself as a professional, and the information posted on these sites can give others an indication of who you are. Some people choose to have a professional account in which all things presented are related to work and professional relationships, and they also have a personal account that is developed under another name that is shared only with personal friends and family. Using social media appropriately can help you develop an understanding of your co-workers and other professionals while also keeping you apprised of important workplace events, but using these sites in an irresponsible way may make others view you in a negative light.

A method of communication that will most likely increase as you enter the workforce is communicating through email. Most formal and informal communication at work will be done through email, so it is vital to not only check your email, but to respond to emails often. Although communicating through email is fairly technical, the tone and message is still important. A well-written email will not only get your point across clearly, but can also give a good impression of you as a professional.

Table 7.1 Different ways of communicating in the workplace

	Face-to-face		Email		Phone call		Texting		Social media	
	Supervisors	Co-workers	Supervisors	Co-workers	Supervisors	Co-workers	Supervisors	Co-workers	Supervisors	Co-workers
Co-worker isn't at work	Yes	Yes	No	No	Yes	Yes	No	Yes	No	No
Running late for work	No	No	Yes	Yes	Yes	Yes	No	Yes	No	No
You wake up sick	No	No	Yes	Yes	Yes	No	No	Yes	No	No
You have an emergency	No	No	No	No	Yes	Yes	Yes	Yes	No	No
Death in the family	Yes	Yes	Yes	Yes	Yes	Yes	No	Yes	No	No
Poor weather conditions	No	No	No	No	Yes	Yes	No	Yes	No	No
Car trouble	No	No	No	No	Yes	Yes	No	Yes	No	No

Planning after-work trivia quiz on Wednesdays	Yes	Yes	Yes	Yes	Yes	Yes	Yes	Yes	Yes	Yes
Co-workers not pulling their weight with a task	Yes	Yes	No	No	No	No	No	No	No	No
Reporting a discrepancy	Yes	Yes	Yes	Yes	Yes	No	No	No	No	No
Talking about a co-worker's birthday party	Yes	No	No	No	No	No	Yes	No	No	No
Asking for a raise/ promotion	Yes	No	No	No	No	No	No	No	No	No
Asking for details of company social event	No	Yes	Yes	No	Yes	No	Yes	No	No	Yes
Submitting your resignation	Yes	No	No	No	No	No	No	No	No	No

A few things to remember when composing an email include the following:

- Use the correct salutation based on your relationship (do not communicate with your boss in the same tone as you would a friend).

- Use a clear and defining statement in the subject line that unmistakably outlines the intention of the email.

- Keep the email to a length of one screen.

- Use proper writing styles with paragraphs and bulleted lists when appropriate.

- Always maintain a courteous tone.

- End the email with a concluding statement that offers direction for the next steps or action.

- Choose an appropriate closing.

- Reread the email before sending it.

- Refrain from writing something that you would not say in person.

- Remember that all email messages can be retrieved.

Jokes are often a way for co-workers to engage in informal conversation and to share time, but this is a difficult area to navigate. The punch lines are often tied to subtle nuances. This, along with the difficulty that individuals with ASD may have with understanding sarcasm, could create a situation in which others are laughing and the person with ASD is left out due to not understanding the context. Jokes can also be very offensive if the content is political, religious, or sexual in nature. If you tell a joke to someone who has a different religious belief system or political viewpoint, you may offend them and cause them to not want to engage with you professionally or personally. People occasionally withhold direct feedback about things that have offended them to avoid creating conflict. Instead, they do not laugh, they offer subtle non-verbal cues that they are offended, or turn and walk away from you without saying anything. Without the direct feedback that the other person was offended, a person with ASD could tell an off-color joke again, creating another incidence of feeling offended. At this time, a co-worker may then go to HR and tell them that you have created a hostile work environment for them, which could result in a written report, departmental transfer, suspension, or even termination. You should also avoid telling jokes with sexual content. These jokes can be very funny if told to the right person with whom you have a personal relationship and have agreed that these jokes are acceptable. If told to a co-worker who has not agreed, telling these jokes could create a highly volatile work environment. The recipient of the joke may then choose to report you to HR for sexual harassment, which could result in termination and a negative stamp on your resume for the rest of your career. If you choose to engage in telling jokes, the best approach to navigate telling jokes with colleagues is to avoid these three mentioned topics, and only tell jokes that would be acceptable to children and to families.

An aspect of peer-to-peer interaction in the workforce that could have a significantly negative impact on the career of professionals with ASD is difficulty in understanding co-workers' subtle social cues, understanding others' viewpoints, and understanding the unspoken social rules of the workplace and obsessive behaviors focused on individuals, which could increase the likelihood that individuals with ASD may engage in what is referred to as "unintentional stalking" (Post *et al.* 2014). Post *et al.* (2014) further describe unintentional stalking as misinterpreting social cues that signal unwanted contact. Stalking is a behavior that may not only cause a person to lose his or her job, but can also become a legal issue, so it is important to develop a set of rules to be followed consistently to avoid this potential outcome.

In the workplace, there is a fine line between professional and personal communication. While it may be acceptable to ask a co-worker to join you for lunch, asking that same co-worker to go out for dinner together could be viewed as a request for a date. It may be acceptable to ask a co-worker out on a date, but if the co-worker is uncomfortable with this, he or she may not be direct in offering that information, but instead, will not respond. You may also discover a co-worker with a shared interest who may be an interesting person to have as a friend. A professional with ASD may ask that person to do something social that is unrelated to work. Again, this is an acceptable thing to do, and if the co-worker doesn't share the same interest in developing a friendship, he or she may not be direct in that feedback. It is when an individual with ASD continues to engage in conversations that trouble may arise. It may not be the intention of the individual with ASD to engage in stalking behaviors, but the co-worker may feel very uncomfortable and unsafe.

To successfully navigate social interactions in the workplace and to avoid potential pitfalls, it is useful to create a set of social rules of your own. Among these, some key things to consider are the content of conversations, number of contact attempts, and interpreting responses:

- Until you have an established personal relationship with another person and have agreed to acceptable content of conversations, do not engage in any conversations that include sexual content. Engaging in sexual conversations with a co-worker without such agreed acceptance may result in immediate termination from your job.

- If you have made contact with a co-worker and the co-worker doesn't respond, it is acceptable to make an additional contact asking for clarification, but do not make any more attempts to contact the co-worker after this. You should consider a "no response" a negative response, and don't make further contact until the co-worker contacts you in return.

- If you have received a response from a co-worker but you are unclear about the intent, ask the co-worker directly rather than making an assumption. Asking for clarification from the other person will allow you to understand more completely, and should keep you out of legal difficulties.

A method for creating this professional social rulebook would be to create a notecard system such as the following example:

If:	Meaning:	Then:
• My co-worker does not respond to my request for a date	• My co-worker may not have received the message • My co-worker may not be interested in a date with me • My co-worker may still be deciding on an answer	• Send one message asking if he or she received the message, and don't send any other messages until I receive a response

FIGURE 7.1 NOTECARD SYSTEM

Tips for peer-to-peer interactions:

- Avoid volatile topics.

- Maintain a professional tone in all communication.

- Be mindful of the responses from co-workers and seek clarification when needed.

- Develop a set of professional rules.

ENVIRONMENTAL SENSITIVITIES

Hyper- or hyposensitivity to environmental factors is particularly impactful for individuals with ASD. Although these sensory sensitivities are woven within the restricted and repetitive behaviors prong of the DSM-5 (*Diagnostic and Statistical Manual*, 5th edition) diagnosing criteria, these sensitivities can be among the most debilitating factors (Grapel *et al.* 2015) for professionals with ASD. This is an area that is often misunderstood by neurotypical peers, so developing a way to communicate about these needs and advocating for tools to mitigate the effect of the professional environment is the most responsible way to manage this.

Environmental sensitivities can be tied to any of the five senses. If a person has an environmental sensitivity to sound, it is possible that a co-worker tapping on the keys on a keyboard could sound like a person banging on a drum next to their head. If a person has a heightened sensitivity to smell, a co-worker popping popcorn in a microwave could cause intense headaches and nausea for a person with ASD. If a person has a heightened sensitivity to light, the florescent lights often used in offices to save energy could cause migraines and loss of focus. If a person has a heightened sensitivity to the texture of foods, trying food that a colleague brings into the office could result in gagging and inadvertently offending the colleague. As an individual with ASD you are the expert on the individual impact these environmental issues have on your work capacity.

The tools and strategies used to mitigate the impact of these sensitivities can be immensely helpful, but if not communicated to your colleagues, these same tools can isolate you from the rest of the work team. For example, if you have a heightened sensitivity to sound, you may choose to wear headphones to filter out the office chatter. While this may be a great solution for you personally, you could miss out on conversations around you or people may avoid attempting to talk with you because you are wearing headphones. By posting a sign on your door that states "I'm wearing headphones so I can concentrate. If you need to talk with me, please tap my desk and let me know," you will allow co-workers to know that you are open to having conversations, and this gives them a method for alerting you of the need to talk with you.

Another environmental factor that could have a potential impact on your work is that of lighting sensitivity. Many offices use fluorescent lighting, which has little impact on the majority of workers. For those with environmental sensitivities, the flickering of the lights, the hum created by the lights, and the other sounds around them could be enough strain on the central nervous system that a person with ASD could feel intense physical pain. A good tool to use that can mitigate this impact would be to ask for lamps as an accommodation. If this is not possible, wearing sunglasses may be effective in calming the flickering of the lights. Again, making colleagues aware of why you are wearing sunglasses inside should limit any negative perceptions.

Finally, because workplaces are becoming so infused with office chatter and non-work-related conversations as a way to build teams, a potential for avoiding sensory overload is to request a specific location for your office or workspace. Many businesses now have collaborative workspaces or shared work pods instead of individual offices. In this effort to design work environments and to create stronger work teams, professionals with ASD are being consistently challenged. As the expert in the impact of environmental sensitivities, it is well within your rights to request to have your workspace located away from the break room, cafeteria, or conference room. By explaining to your supervisor the potentially negative impact of environmental factors within your control, he or she may be willing to allow you to choose your workspace location. This self-advocacy will not only allow you to have control over your environment and potentially avoid a meltdown due to sensory overload, but will also help those around you understand this very real consequence.

Tips for environmental sensitivities:

- Understand the impact the work environment has on you as an individual.

- Advocate for the tools you need to mitigate the impact.

- Educate colleagues about the impact of environmental sensitivities on you.

- Explain why you need tools for dealing with your environmental sensitivities.

LESSON 2: LEARNING THROUGH CASUAL INTERACTIONS

Informal office gatherings can include holiday parties hosted by the company, lunch gatherings, Friday afternoon drinks, or occasional shared lunch times. While these gatherings are often optional and do not directly affect the job as defined, they do serve a purpose. These times together are when colleagues develop trusting relationships with each other, which helps build morale on the job.

Because these gatherings are not required, professionals with ASD often opt out of attending. The social nature of these gatherings can be overwhelming, and if there is no direct link to job performance, the value in the experience may be lost. But opting out of all of these experiences may place those with ASD at the outside of the work circle. By not taking advantage of these opportunities to make connections, co-workers may feel that they are not engaged members of the work team.

Holiday gatherings are often a way for companies to offer their thanks to the employees, while also encouraging the development of camaraderie. These opportunities are for supervisors and workers to engage in conversations that may be less formal, while also offering insights into life outside of work. This is a time when teams may talk about vacation plans, family members, future goals, etc. This is a great time to share with others any future goals you may have, and you may find that others share the same goals. This is also a time when your supervisors can get to know what is important to you. Of all the potential informal gatherings, these holiday gatherings are the ones professionals with ASD should make every attempt to attend.

Some things to consider regarding taking part in holiday gatherings include the level of expectations on participants. If the gathering is a "potluck" and the expectation is that everyone will bring a dish to share with others, whether you choose to eat at the party or not, you must still being something to share. Many individuals with ASD have significant food intolerances, so they choose to not eat at these gatherings, but it may be interpreted as rude to come to a party and to not bring a dish to share. Also consider the location of the gathering, as this will often dictate the dress required. If a party is more formal, the expected level of dress will often be outlined in the invitation, but if the party is held at work or at a person's house, it is safe to dress "business casual." This will alleviate the potential for you to show up overdressed or underdressed for the occasion.

Conversations at these gatherings tend to be more informal, and it is possible for individuals with ASD to monopolize conversations without realizing it. Keep in mind that these times are for everyone to engage in conversations, so monitor your time talking, and be sure to allow others to talk at least as much as you. Finally, these gatherings are a time to celebrate together, so it is important to avoid engaging in negative conversations or complaining about office issues.

Consistent shared lunch times are also times to engage in building relationships with co-workers. These lunches are not required and are typically not arranged by a supervisor, but emerge as a tradition experienced by co-workers. An example of this type of gathering could be "Taco Tuesdays" in which every Tuesday colleagues go to lunch together at a local Mexican restaurant. Because of potential food intolerances, individuals with ASD may opt out of these lunches, but this should not be the only reason to decline. An option to eat your preferred food while still engaging in this informal gathering would be to eat the lunch you bring from home prior to the gathering, then simply get a drink and engage in conversations with your colleagues.

While these gatherings are informal and have no direct impact on your job, it is recommended that you engage in these opportunities at least occasionally. Although you may tend to prefer a structured routine, occasionally attending these lunches will allow you to become a valued member of the work team, and will encourage the team to continue to invite you to participate.

Friday afternoon drinks or occasional lunch invitations also serve a purpose, but of all the informal gatherings, these are the ones that have the least impact. Some work teams refer to this as going to "happy hour" or "Friday afternoon club," and use these opportunities to decompress from the working week and to get ready for the weekend. You may not drink alcohol, but participating in these opportunities does have value for building relationships. And you can attend without consuming alcohol. Occasional lunch invitations signify that co-workers value the relationship with you, and this should also be considered. Valued work relationships are encouraging and help people feel accepted and respected in the workplace. If an individual consistently turns down lunch invitations, they will no longer be invited to join the work team for these informal gatherings. While engaging in these optional and informal gatherings can be taxing on your social energy, they are important in solidifying your position in a work team. To develop and maintain a sense of community with co-workers, try to participate in these opportunities as often as possible.

While these opportunities are important and serve as an avenue for building a community with your work partners, it is also important to monitor your personal levels of social energy. Individuals with ASD tend to expend a significant amount of energy when participating in social gatherings. Spending too much social energy on these opportunities without allowing for adequate time to recharge may result in diminished social energy, mental clarity, and focus on the job. Setting personal boundaries and sticking to them should help you manage social opportunities while also maintaining your health and wellness. Refer to previous chapters to develop strategies, resources, and professional tools to best manage the potential impact of engaging in social gatherings.

Individuals with ASD have often been described as being analytical and academic observers (Rigler *et al.* 2015c). This strength associated with ASD can help professionals become successful in the workplace. By taking a sociological approach to understanding the water cooler culture of the workplace, you can potentially develop a detailed understanding of the unspoken social rules of the work setting.

People with ASD often recognize the fine details in situations that are overlooked by others. This can help individuals make sense of the social rules required to belong in the culture of the workplace. While it is not the expectation that professionals with ASD must change themselves to fit in, it is notable that developing an understanding of the details of the culture can help avoid any social faux pas. By combining fine attention to detail and keen observation skills, you can take an academic approach to observing and documenting the detail of the interactions between co-workers. Following an interaction with colleagues, make note of the specific details of the interaction and any questions that may arise as a result. Compare the details within the interaction, and make connections when possible. Continue this method until you feel comfortable in developing a professional social rule to guide future interactions with your co-workers. To ensure that the rules you establish are, in fact, correct, elicit the support of a work mentor who can help you understand the social structure.

This method could lend itself to another strength associated with many individuals with ASD. If rules are developed and the purpose is understood, a person with ASD will likely follow those rules and be uncomfortable deviating from them. This could allow people with ASD to begin to understand and navigate the social rules that may not be overtly discussed. Developing your own set of professional social rules based on observations can provide more credibility to those rules than if another colleague simply tells you an expectation. By basing rule development on observed interactions and outcomes, the purpose becomes clear, and can be adhered to.

Another strength that can be used to navigate the water cooler culture of the workplace is associated with honesty. People with ASD tend to be honest and not easily led (Rigler *et al.* 2015b), which can be viewed as a break from the norm in a potentially gossip-filled political work environment. While professionals with ASD are authentic in their interactions, they may not pick up on the fact that others are not as forthcoming. This could cause social confusion, particularly in the less formal conversations during down time; however, many people with ASD prefer honest feedback from others as well. While neurotypical people tend to respond to critical feedback with some level of emotion, professionals with ASD tend to thrive on that level of direct feedback and respect those providing that directness. This desire to receive direct feedback can make employees with ASD constantly improving employees who take responsibility for their professional growth.

LESSON 3: JOINING IN THE CULTURE

The informal and unspoken social nuances of the work environment are often what negatively impacts the ability for professionals with ASD to maintain employment. Because the difficulties associated with ASD lie with developing meaning from context and understanding social cues, these ever-changing social rules create immense confusion in the work setting. These are not only informal and unspoken, but the expectations shift from situation to situation and from person to person, also making them inconsistent and unpredictable.

Use the following scenarios regarding the water cooler culture within the work environment to begin developing your own set of professional social rules. Evaluate how the people in the scenarios managed the interactions, and use their experiences to guide your professional development.

PATRICIA'S STORY

Patricia was new to a large insurance company and served on a large team of accountants. When she was hired, her direct supervisor told her that they were making a shift as part of the company's new mission to become more collaborative and team-based. She was slightly concerned about this arrangement because working on teams had never been easy for her, but her supervisor was very excited about this initiative, and she was afraid that if she said she was concerned, she would not get the job, so she acted as excited as he was.

During her first week on the job, Patricia settled in and met her team. The team was made up of three other accountants with vastly different backgrounds and experiences. Each of the team members shared information about their education, work history, family, and personal information in an attempt to get to know each other. Although she knew it was important to do so, Patricia was not yet comfortable sharing her ASD diagnosis with them.

This team of four professionals shared a work pod, which can be described as a large office cubicle with four desks that were connected and that face each other. Their work pod was located right next to the break room which had a refrigerator, water cooler, coffee pot, and a microwave, to be used by everyone. The other members of the team were happy with this location, but Patricia could only see the difficulties it could create—this would be where everyone would take time away from work, creating unnecessary chatter right outside their workspace, people would cook their meals creating unpleasant smells, people would walk by their door, constantly creating distractions. This could all detract from the work that Patricia was hired to do. Although she was concerned, she kept this feeling to herself so she wasn't seen as a complainer.

After the first month as a part of this work team, coming to work was almost unbearable for Patricia. One of her partners came to work with incredibly strong cologne on every day, which gave her intense headaches, the chatter coming from the break room felt as loud to her as a jack hammer in her head, and another of her partners popped popcorn and ate it at their work pod every day at 2.00pm. She chewed with her mouth open and crunched the popcorn incessantly for no less than 30 minutes. One afternoon Patricia felt like she was approaching sensory overload and could no longer filter any of the environmental stimuli of the office setting. As her partner sat down and began chewing on her popcorn, Patricia stood up and began screaming at her. She called her a cow and said that the sound of her chewing made her want to punch her in the face. Then she ran out of the office and went directly home to her dark, quiet apartment.

The next day, Patricia was called into HR for a meeting with her supervisor and the HR manager. She was written up for being aggressive to her partner and creating a hostile work environment. She was told that if it happened again, her contract would be terminated.

What would have been a better way for Patricia to join this work team?

_____

_____

_____

_____

_____

What were the major issues that caused difficulties for Patricia in the new work setting?

_____

_____

_____

_____

_____

What would Patricia need to tell the HR manager and her supervisor to avoid her contract being terminated?

_____

_____

_____

_____

_____

STEPHEN'S STORY

Stephen had been working in the engineering firm for approximately eight months, and had been doing his job with little difficulty. He had minor issues with his co-workers, and sometimes people got irritated with him, but he didn't understand why. It seemed to him like they all had a different employee handbook than he did, and they all knew and followed a different set of rules. Nobody really wanted to talk to him, so he just focused on his job and did his work very well.

A new engineer recently joined the firm. Her name was Sara and she was very nice to Stephen. She occasionally sat with him at lunch, and when other co-workers were rude to him, she stood up for him. She talked to him about her weekend plans, and showed him pictures of her dog. Stephen thought that maybe she was interested in him as a friend, or maybe more.

Stephen sat down with Sara for lunch one day and began asking her about her plans for the upcoming weekend. She talked about taking her dog on a hike and going to find some waterfalls just outside of town. Stephen then said, "I was thinking about going out for pizza on Saturday night, would you like to join me? We could maybe go see a movie after?"

Sara responded to his request by telling him that she already had plans, but thanks for asking. She then left and went back to work. Stephen thought of another idea so he texted her another request saying, "I know you have plans on Saturday, but my family is having a barbeque on Sunday, would you like to join us for that?"

Sara again responded that she already had plans and would not be able to make it.

Stephen continued to request time with Sara outside of work hours so they could get to know each other, but they could never find a time that worked for her. She seemed to always have plans, but she never told him "no," so he tried again and again, through emails, text messages, and when they passed each other in the office.

Sara stopped having lunch with Stephen but he didn't understand why. He didn't see her as much around the firm, and was concerned about her, so he started calling her to see if she was okay or if she was upset with him for something. She didn't answer his phone calls for an entire week, so he began texting her many times every day. If she would just let him know what he had done, he could fix it, but she didn't respond.

Finally, Stephen saw Sara leaving the office heading to the parking lot, so he went after her to try to talk to her. As he was walking to the parking lot, Stephen was forming his script in his mind so he would say the right thing. He didn't notice that he had started running toward Sara until he saw that she had got into her car and locked the door before driving off quickly.

The next day, Stephen was put on administrative leave pending an investigation for stalking Sara and making her afraid to come to work. He was devastated because that was not what he had intended at all; he was just confused and she had never told him "no."

What created the confusion for Stephen?

_____

_____

_____

_____

_____

What limits should Stephen have set for himself?

_____

_____

_____

_____

_____

What possible consequences could Stephen face as a result of this social confusion?

_____

_____

_____

_____

_____

HARRY'S STORY

Harry had been working as a chemistry professor at a medium-sized public university for approximately ten years. He was very good at chemistry and knew a lot about his area, but he had received some complaints from his students about his communication style. They claimed that he was harsh in his conversations, and when they asked for help, he made them feel stupid for not understanding. People had said that before about Harry, but he attributed the confusion to his ASD diagnosis and dismissed it. His department head told him that if he wanted to achieve tenure, he would need to research more and partner with the other faculty members in his department on presentations. He wanted to achieve tenure from this university, so he knew he had to make some changes.

Harry didn't know much about the other faculty members in his department, even after ten years of working with them. Before he could propose partnering on research and presentations, he knew he had to get to know them better as individuals. He didn't want to partner with someone who would drag him down or make him do all the work. Harry had always felt that he was the most knowledgeable faculty member in the chemistry department, so he needed to find a partner who could match his intelligence.

The annual university holiday party was coming up in the week, so Harry decided that it was a good place to start to get to know the others better. He had always viewed these parties as a waste of time, but this year there was a purpose for attending. He planned to go to the party to discuss some options for research with some of his colleagues and also so that the department head could see that he was making an effort.

On the day of the party, Harry got dressed in his regular clothing that he wore every day and went to the party. When he arrived, he noticed everyone had brought food to share and they were dressed up. Harry didn't know he was supposed to bring something to share, and he also didn't know that he was supposed to dress up, so he immediately became upset that nobody had told him these were the expectations. He joined the party anyway, and found a seat next to one of his colleagues who was already engaged in a conversation with someone about their holiday plans.

Harry listened while his colleague chatted about things that he viewed as meaningless, and he waited for a break in the conversation. When his colleague stopped talking for a minute, he immediately started talking with her about research. He told her, "Apparently students don't like how I talk to them, sensitive babies, and boss man said I need to do more research and presentations with someone else from out department. I definitely don't make enough money now and really need to get tenured so you are the chosen one. I have this great idea for research and already have started. Want to attach your name and call it done?"

Harry's colleague walked away from him and sat at another table with another group of people from the department. Harry sat by himself for the rest of the party. Nobody wanted to partner with him on research and he did not make tenure that year.

What unspoken social rules did Harry break?

_____

_____

_____

_____

_____

How could Harry have better approached colleagues about partnering on research?

_____

_____

_____

_____

_____

How could Harry respond to the feedback from students about his communication style?

_____

_____

_____

_____

_____

LESSON 4: PROFESSIONAL TOOL FOR CREATING SOCIAL RULES

Due to the unpredictability and inconsistent nature of the rules associated with this water cooler culture in the workplace, individuals with ASD must develop strategies to help navigate this confusing aspect of employment. While there is no evidence-based approach to navigating these unspoken social rules that neurotypical workers understand intuitively, professionals with ASD can develop a rulebook to help them overcome this confusion. While it may continue to be difficult to generalize the rules to other interactions, developing these professional social rules may offer some degree of understanding to help mute some of the social confusion and lessen the potential for professional isolation or loss of employment due to breaking these social rules.

The following example of a rule card outlines a responsible approach to developing a rulebook. This can be a set of index cards, a journal, or an electronic file that can be added to and edited at any time. These social rules are ever-changing and situation-dependent, but developing a rule for interactions can give a professional with ASD a starting point to understanding workplace culture.

Rules should be developed following the observation of an interaction and the connections of the details of these interactions. By combining the details of the interaction with the potential purpose of the rule, a professional with ASD can make a strong commitment to adhering to these professional social rules. While it is difficult to generalize these social rules, outlining potential variations of the rules can offer a framework for assisting with workplace interactions.

The world of work is a confusing place to be. There are many unspoken social rules, and if broken, these social miscues can cause those with ASD to lose their job. Spend time developing a set of professional social rules, and review them consistently. Continue building your rulebook to use as a guide for these social situations at work. It is highly recommended that you develop these rules in partnership with a professional mentor with whom you can check these rules for legitimacy prior to commiting to them, and who understands the confusion you may experience. This should allow for the development of rules that are accurate and appropriate for the professional setting.

Details of the interaction:

Rule:

Purpose of the rule:

Consequence of breaking the rule:

Variations on the rule:

Professional partner:

BACK TO BASICS

B **Behavior** 1 2 3		Do you understand what is meant by company culture? Are you controlling your responses in your professional world? Are you actively seeking new opportunities?
A **Academics** 1 2 3		Are you completing your task? Are you asking for clarification regarding expectations at work? Is your role defined within the team?
S **Self-care** 1 2 3		Are you sleeping? Are you following through with your wellness plan? Are you maintaining age-appropriate hygiene? Are you taking time to engage in activities outside of your professional work? Are you communicating your needs or points of confusion with others?
I **Interaction** 1 2 3		Are you engaging in small talk with co-workers? Are you planning time for social activities? Are you having a positive or negative impact on those you work with?
C **Community** 1 2 3		Is your work environment a good fit? Do you feel like you belong? Do you know the names of your co-workers?
S **Self-monitoring** 1 2 3		Are you accepting and using feedback? Are you managing your frustration levels? Are you monitoring your interactions for appropriateness?

GOALS

Personal:

Aptitude:

Social:

BACK TO BASICS: RATE YOURSELF

		Comments
B	**Behavior** 1 2 3	Comments
A	**Academics** 1 2 3	Comments
S	**Self-care** 1 2 3	Comments
I	**Interaction** 1 2 3	Comments
C	**Community** 1 2 3	Comments
S	**Self- monitoring** 1 2 3	Comments

GOALS

Personal:

Aptitude:

Social:

Chapter 8

PROFESSIONAL GROWTH

INTRODUCTION

Professional development, according to Bissonnette (2013), is two-fold: first, professionals must learn, practice, and sharpen the skills they demonstrate at their job each day; and second, young professionals should maintain an awareness of trends in their job field. Day-to-day workplace aptitude is a considerable element of professional development. Many workshops, webinars, and presentations are geared toward improving employees' practical skills. When it comes to staying aware of current trends in the field, however, you will need to put in some personal effort. With some research, you should be able to access information about professional associations, community interest groups, blogs, and academic journal articles. Some workplaces facilitate their employees' access to these professional development opportunities and tools.

Those with ASD in the workplace will benefit from regular professional development. Learning and practicing more about the field in order to progress through it is a linear and logical concept. As young professionals gain skills and experience, their value as employees increases. Likewise, if professional development is avoided or not given adequate attention, young professionals with ASD may fall behind at work compared to their co-workers.

Learning that fresh starts are normal is one goal of this chapter, while another is to make you aware of the opportunities that you will have available as a young professional for your professional growth and development.

LESSON 1: STARTING OVER IS OKAY

With your focus on career advancement, you will likely critically evaluate your current status and assess your satisfaction and progress in the workplace. What this evaluation looks like will depend on how you perceive your present status in your career, and what your future career goals are. If you are nearing graduation from college, this could involve considering practical and logistic factors such as where, or if, you are willing to move to pursue a position. If you are a part-time employee or in an internship, you may think about whether or not the experience you have gained in your support role has impacted your career interests. As a new professional in an entry-level position in your desired field, your evaluation should be especially critical of the degree to which you have professional and personal fit in your job. These considerations are simply part of professional growth.

As a young adult continuing to orient yourself in the workplace, understand that finding yourself in a bad professional fit and deciding to start over may be a reasonable solution. Keep in mind, though, that the very nature of starting over involves significant change and transition, which often challenges those on the spectrum. Transitions can offer new platforms for you to demonstrate all the skills you have acquired through previous experience and professional development. Furthermore, it is unrealistic to assume that as a recent college graduate you will be maintaining your first professional position indefinitely. As you progress further into your field, a process that will certainly involve both failures and successes, you will be able to learn from and respond to prior pitfalls with more professional insight and experience to boost your confidence in your readiness for a different position.

Whether you are interested in furthering your responsibility at your current workplace or if you are in a position to seek new employment elsewhere, your day-to-day work is simply one part of your responsibility as a young professional. Employment is not guaranteed to last for anyone, even if your work output is impeccable. Company goals, budgets, and leadership changes shifts priorities for employment needs. Likewise, your own goals, budget, and lifestyle changes will shift your employment priorities. Due to this uncertainty and the subsequent need to maintain your marketability as an employee, engage in professional development.

Young adults with ASD will need to consider the potential challenges of professional development. One possible challenge is that professional development involves learning about, adapting to, and working in an environment that has layers of unspoken rules for social norms in the workplace that, especially for those with ASD, complicates the task of maintaining productive work output and finding social fit. Fostering relationships with colleagues within the field is to the employed young professional what seeking various networking contacts in the community is to the aspiring job applicant. Social relationships are tied to professional development in this way.

Young professionals should keep in mind that entry-level jobs, such as some office administrative support positions, generally require employees to interact daily with co-workers and/or clients, be adaptable, and work in a sensory-filled environment (Hendrickx 2009). After college, many first positions that graduates apply for and receive are those that demand the very skills that challenge many young adults with ASD. Employment, even for those with minimal client or customer contact, will nearly always involve working with other people.

In addition to being tasked with interpreting workplace-specific social nuances that seem to come naturally for neurotypical young professionals, having ASD may also impact how you adjust during transitions. Unfortunately for those who do struggle with transitions, there are many in the early career of a typical young professional. First of all, just as entering college is fraught with new environments and responsibilities, for those encountering college graduation, transitioning out of college and into "the real world" is not easy. The routine, structure, and organization systems that you created in college over the course of your academic pursuits no longer readily apply to your post-graduation life. Developing similar kinds of systems, though, in new workplace environments over and over again along your career path is one of the more challenging aspects of professional development.

Interpreting workplace social nuances and adapting to transitional stages of the career progression both involve a common theme in the life of many young professionals. Basically, professional development, for many adults with ASD, involves working outside of their "comfort zone." Growing in your career is often in response to change. As you learn through your experience at work, you become a more advanced and capable employee. For you, this development and professional growth can lead to career advancement. For your employers, your professional growth means you are a more valuable member of the team. Many opportunities for growth, such as attending conferences, presenting at meetings, or adding new responsibilities at work, demand that employees go a little outside of their comfort zone in order to develop professionally.

Starting over in a new position or a new field may or may not be your original idea. Better job positions may open up with a better salary, and this could lead you to move into a new position. Some people move to new cities and must start over at work, or have families that influence what kind of work and/or where they go to work. Even a simple promotion to a new department can feel like you are starting over. You may be fired or let go from one position and move into another to start over. Being aware of and prepared for these realistic possible interferences on your career path will make it easier for you to adapt to new circumstances should you have to start over.

Not every position you have during your career progression will be the right fit. If you are dissatisfied with your work, this can impact all other areas of your life. All professionals go through bouts of dissatisfaction at work, but minor annoyances are different from persistent unhappiness and genuine lack of professional fit. The difference between conflicts impacting work satisfaction is that minor issues, such as having to cover two extra shifts in one week for a sick co-worker, only cause tension for most professionals temporarily. Serious conflict or lasting lack of fulfillment often persistently impact the wellness of professionals until concrete resolution occurs.

New professionals evaluating whether they are in the wrong job or career can use these signals (adapted from a list in Bissonnette 2013) to reflect on their satisfaction and progress at work:

Reflect	Signs	Notes
Do you have difficulty maintaining similar positions?	You have been fired more than once from similar positions for similar reasons; you are changing jobs very frequently for similar reasons	
Are you consistently failing at work tasks because you are disorganized?	You have missed deadlines; your work is rushed and subpar; you lose track of task instructions	
Is your personal wellness taking a toll as a result of work?	You work more hours than co-workers just to keep up; you are constantly exhausted after work; you have little time for engaging with personal interests to relieve stress	
Have you found a social fit in the workplace?	You are engaged in serious interpersonal conflict with co-workers or supervisors; you are isolated and disconnected; you are experiencing harassment or bullying at work	

In the space below, note down individual and specific aspects of your professional development and the process of improving yourself as an employee that you need to regularly evaluate (e.g. communication, resume maintenance, networking, etc.). Create and write or draw your own workplace cue for addressing it.

If you find that you are seeing these signs of a bad fit at work, you will need to develop a plan of action. Results from direct approaches such as asking for clarification on an issue bothering you at work, or trying new approaches to problems that once seemed unsolvable will help you determine whether or not you have given your dilemma significant consideration.

Impulsively quitting your job will make it more difficult to find a new one in the future. Keep in mind that part of your plan could simply be to give the situation at work a little time. Even if you have made the decision to quit your job, give yourself some time to prepare for your next step. In many cases, young professionals seeking out employment positions will still be employed, and once an offer is made for another position, the employee will resign from their current one to pursue the new one. Giving your employers notice of your intention to resign is common courtesy.

Since companies seeking to hire will be interested in the previous employment circumstances of their applicants, those that ended on poor terms (such as immediate dismissal or sudden resignation) are likely to have a more difficult time in the job search process. If you are dissatisfied at work and are considering your options, even if you do not end up taking another position, the process of searching for potential employment opportunities that interest you can keep you up-to-date on current position requirements. This knowledge will help you design a professional development plan that is aimed at improving the aspects of your employment that need to be improved.

LESSON 2: ONGOING PROFESSIONAL DEVELOPMENT

As a young professional, you will develop into a more marketable job applicant and a more prepared and skilled employee by intentionally seeking career-advancing opportunities and staying aware of progression in your field.

This effort, generally referred to as "professional development," requires diligent work. It typically occurs in coordination with or in addition to an employment position. The purpose of engaging in professional development opportunities as a young professional is essentially to consistently improve your employability—both as a currently employed professional and as a future candidate for a career-advancing position. Professional development occurs through an employee's direct actions. It is intentional effort toward bettering oneself as an employee and/or potential employee.

Five essential components summarize professional development for young adults: progress, adaptation, participation, awareness, and evaluation. Individually, these components can certainly influence your professional growth. Putting effort into each component should lead to comprehensive professional development. Of these five elements, some applications, particularly adaptation and participation, are especially challenging for those on the spectrum. Balancing your effort between mastering the different components of professional development will prepare you for a wider range of opportunity.

Read through the following descriptors of the five professional development components, and use the prompts in the chart to assess your own professional efforts.

Progress: In order to advance in your career and move forward, young professionals must experience progress. One goal of professional development should be to progress through learning, seeing, or doing something to ensure growth between beginning and transition out of a position.

Notes:

_____

_____

Adaptation: Improving professional employability as a young professional occurs in part as a result of transition and the employee's responsibility to adapt. As professionals gain more experience and knowledge, their career intentions may change and they will have to adapt their course to meet new goals. As employment needs change, employees may have to adapt to new responsibilities or new leadership.

Notes:

_____

_____

Participation: Professional development does not occur passively. Young professionals grow through their actions. Participating, contributing to both productive and social goals of the workplace, is essential.

Notes:

_____

_____

Awareness: In addition to keeping up with day-to-day workplace duties, young professionals must stay aware of trends in their fields. This involves individual efforts (such as reading applicable studies/new articles) and working within the broad range of the field (such as attending conferences). Awareness connects employees to their purpose at work as well as to the shared experiences of those who do similar jobs.

Notes:

_____

_____

Evaluation: Assessing progress and fitness for a position in order to make educated career decisions is essential to professional development. Knowing how well employees are meeting expectations at the workplace allows them to direct their goals. Evaluation leads young professionals to know their strengths, weaknesses, and more adeptly consider their interests and capability in a position or career field.

Notes:

_____

_____

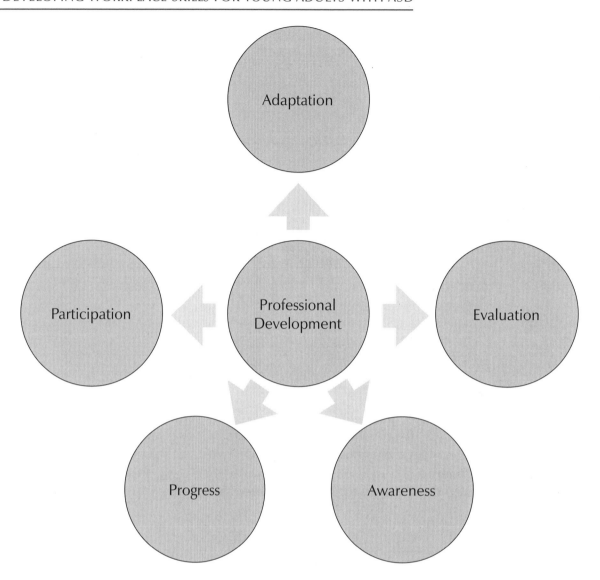

FIGURE 8.1 FIVE COMPONENTS OF PROFESSIONAL DEVELOPMENT

These five elements of professional development may be gathered through opportunities built into the workplace structure or through individual efforts. While some employers value and encourage professional development opportunities even to the point of funding an employee's access to these, other employers have little to do directly with the employee's additional professional development. Setting your own goals for professional development and sharing them with someone aware of your career interests will help hold you accountable.

Keep in mind a few logistical points about pursuing professional development. First, remember that your appearance and dress requirements will also likely fluctuate in response to shifts in responsibility and status at work. When you attend professional development gatherings, your appearance and dress will be considered by potential networking contacts. You will be expected to engage in small talk and demonstrate interest and ability in work-related topics. This overall professional demeanor is often developed through exposure to these kinds of professional development opportunities.

Professional development opportunities include graduate school or other advanced certificates, volunteer work, community project work, presentations, and even learning about work culture. To improve your marketability as an employee, you might attend graduate school to get another academic degree. You may find interests and organizations in the community that allow you to hold leadership roles to improve that skill at work. Professional development doesn't always occur through formal and job-specific opportunities, but also through those opportunities you create for yourself to improve some aspect of your career.

This development process, specifically for those with ASD, is assisted by the possession of the many strengths characterized by those with ASD. Professional development demands that employees are persistent enough to continue to work through tough times and confusion. The process also demands that individuals are resourceful and capable of solving complex problems. Individuals with ASD are characterized by their persistence, problem-solving ability, and resourcefulness. These attributes will be incredibly important as you progress through a career. When issues arise at work, you can use your strengths to create a solution, and your work will not be deterred by recurring problems.

In addition to persistence, resourcefulness, and the ability to creatively solve problems to improve outcomes, individuals with ASD are also characterized by their honesty and their possession of intense special interests. When it comes to professional development, these strengths are especially useful. For instance, being honest with yourself and your co-workers about your challenges will help you notice the areas you can improve through professional development. The special interests you have, especially if they are tied to the work you do or seek to do, are motivation to consider additional experience and further growth. They can influence your career field, of course, but these interests may also lead you to gain skills through community engagement in your interest area. Professional development will be ongoing, challenging, and frustrating, and individuals with ASD can particularly struggle with its social elements.

Despite these challenges, though, it will prove to be an influential process for all young professionals, especially those with ASD who have the complementary strengths necessary to take advantage of the benefits.

LESSON 3: EVALUATION AND FEEDBACK

Young professionals in the workplace can expect their performance to be evaluated regularly. In fact, evaluations of your performance and fit will occur even as early as the interview phase. Part of your supervisor's responsibility will be to ensure you are trained and prepared for your own duties. Evaluations at work may be formal and routine, or they may be more informal and infrequent. Some occupations require regular evaluations for employees to be considered for a promotion or a salary raise. Informal types of evaluation could simply occur as your supervisor walks around the office, observing employees' work ethic.

Evaluation gives information about your performance that can then be addressed through feedback. While those with ASD may prefer direct feedback, your supervisor may be less assertive and clear when offering feedback. If this is the case, and your supervisor's vague feedback is making it difficult for you to assess your performance, ask for clarification. Once your preference for direct feedback is known, it may take off some of the pressure of the person giving you feedback. There may be formal methods of delivering feedback, or it may be given casually. Feedback will include observations about your progress at work, and will make you aware of the areas in which you can improve.

When you receive feedback it is important that you write it down or make a copy of the formal evaluation for your records. You should then be able to notice over time how your evaluations have addressed your growth.

When it comes to individuals with ASD being evaluated and given feedback, some of the workplace social nuances can interfere with the message about work progress. Read through the following scenarios and reflect on the ways the individuals could use their experiences with feedback and evaluation for their professional development.

MAX'S STORY

Max is a veterinary technician who works part-time while attending graduate school. He has been working for the same veterinary doctor for two years, and has gained an understanding of his supervisor's assistance needs and his individual responsibilities as a technician. He disclosed his ASD to the veterinary doctor and received a positive response. His request for direct and regular feedback has proven to be the key to using feedback in his professional development. The veterinary doctor meets with him each Monday morning before the office opens, to go over weekly goals and to discuss any issues from the previous week. This regular feedback has enabled Max to monitor his work productivity and avoid stressing over whether or not he is performing well at work.

The veterinary doctor at Max's office has to take three weeks off to recover from a medical concern. During the doctor's time away, Max was instructed to be the "go-to guy" for the interim veterinary doctor. After one week, working with the new doctor proved to be a challenge for Max. Max could not interpret the new doctor's requests for assistance, and as a result was feeling more and more like a burden instead of an assistant. Receiving no routine feedback from the interim veterinary doctor, Max begins to lose track of his goals at work and his performance is subpar. He is concerned that the interim doctor will persuade the regular doctor that he is not cut out for the job.

What could Max do to break the cycle of poor performance at work?

_____

_____

_____

_____

How do you think this experience will help Max prepare for future unexpected shifts in supervision?

_____

_____

_____

_____

How can Max appropriately ensure that his need for feedback is heard by co-workers?

_____

_____

_____

_____

JENNIFER'S STORY

Jennifer is a second-grade teacher at a highly competitive private elementary school. Her primary source of training involved a graduate degree in education, but she has had limited classroom experience. During orientation, the school's principal told the teachers to expect a minimum of one formal observation per grading period. These formal observations would consider the teacher's score from a rubric designed by the school's elite assessment board. Jennifer's first observation goes horribly. The high-stakes nature of the formal evaluations causes anxiety, and she is distracted and fumbling as she teaches the observed lesson to her students. When the principal calls a private meeting, Jennifer expects the worst. Instead, she is met with a series of positive points from her observation, including her ability to connect with the students in between lessons. Jennifer had not realized that the formal evaluation would include her interpersonal interactions in the classroom in addition to the mastery of delivering her academic lessons. While the feedback from the principal did include elements of the observation that she would need to improve, she was thrilled to know her principal had noticed her connection with the students.

How can Jennifer's first observation experience improve her next one?

_____

_____

_____

_____

Is there a way Jennifer could have found out more about the expectations of the formal observations ahead of time?

_____

_____

_____

_____

What strengths does Jennifer possess in her role as a teacher?

_____

_____

_____

_____

LESLIE'S STORY

Leslie's new job as a financial consultant seems to be exactly the right type of position for her. She will have her own individual office, and will only work face-to-face with clients as needed. Her co-workers have more or less left her alone to adjust to the office, and she closes her door often because of the noise generated by the stairwell outside the door. Her success rate with clients seeking economic wisdom and mathematical talent has been at the top of the staff since her third day. At the end of the first two weeks in the position, Leslie's supervisor asks her to meet for a performance review. In the meeting, Leslie is reprimanded for being disconnected from the staff members in the office. The supervisor has been getting complaints that Leslie is unavailable for consultation because her door is closed. Instead of praising her good work with the clients, the supervisor demands that she find a way to connect with the team. Leslie's concern is that if she engages more socially at work, it will impact her performance, which is what she is paid for. She begins leaving her door open for all but one hour each day, and makes an effort to join the team for lunch every Friday. Her next performance review focuses on her ability to maintain a balance between individual success and being a member of the team.

How did Leslie respond to the feedback in her performance review?

_____

_____

_____

_____

What cues could she have looked for to pick up on her co-workers' dissatisfaction before the review?

_____

_____

_____

_____

Why do you think evaluations consider social fit as well as performance?

_____

_____

_____

_____

Young professionals in the workplace will be inundated with opportunities for professional growth. Receiving feedback from evaluations, both formal and informal, and responding actively to improving based on the feedback is a mark of a mature young professional. As someone with ASD, evaluation and feedback will provide you with guidance to improve your work experience.

LESSON 4: PROFESSIONAL TOOLS FOR CONTINUING DEVELOPMENT

Professional development requires young professionals to monitor their productivity during work times on the one hand, and on the other, their adherence to self-care measures to maintain employment. There are constantly new forms of input in the workplace that individuals with ASD have difficulty filtering. Simple self-evaluation tools, such as the pneumonic devices outlined in this lesson, can prompt young professionals with ASD to consider their progress in their current position, and to direct their preparedness measures for future positions. Recalling information through summarized cues for processes and procedures is often demanded by the nature of employment. For example, imagine you have to remember the number seven, the code to clock into work. If you associate that numerical code with something familiar such as a phone number, you will probably more easily remember it. In the case of evaluating your own progress and effort at work, you can benefit from the same concept of simplifying the cues. In this lesson we use two pneumonic devices to offer self-reflecting prompts, but you may prefer to develop other memory cues to ensure you are consistently evaluating your professional development progress.

To ensure that these simple tools are actually practical, you can consider many methods of displaying the cues. You could write them down on sticky-notes for your desk, or write them in a daily planner or journal. Others may prefer to input the cues into a smartphone as the image background or as a reminder. No matter how you organize your cues to make them useful and practical, keep them easy to remember. When work stressors are keeping you from thinking as calmly or as linearly as the situation demands, recalling these cues can assist you in a tough situation.

While you may not wish to complete a lengthy written self-assessment every single day, the following cues are simple enough to be considered daily, with minimal effort. The concept here is simple: recall a word and use the word to guide self-reflection.

First, let's consider the following pneumonic device for assisting you during your evaluation of daily work tasks. The word "work" is used to prompt you to recall and follow through with the actions corresponding with the letters of the word. The idea is that when you are feeling overwhelmed by the immensity of your work tasks and routine, you can see or recall the pneumonic device, and re-gather yourself to get back to work.

W	**Write it down:** Take notes on your tasks
O	**Organize your space:** Keep it clutter-free
R	**Refresh:** Stay focused
K	**Keep up:** Monitor your time and output

Another aspect of professional development besides just keeping up with daily work is ensuring that you are taking care of your personal interests so they do not interfere with work. Work, in addition to the stress of workplace social interpretation, is best handled when breaks are worked in for self-care. As an individual with ASD, the input from all angles of the workplace, especially sensory stimuli, can make it difficult to maintain expected work output standards. Sometimes taking a short break to regroup and tackle tasks after a bit of relaxation can help your approach to issues and problems that you are working on. In the next pneumonic, consider how the word "break" can be used to prompt your self-reflection about appropriate on-the-job self-care.

B	**Brief:** Breaks should be quick
R	**Relaxing:** Get work off your mind
E	**Every day:** Take breaks daily
A	**Alone:** Allow yourself personal time
K	**Know it's okay:** Breaks refocus you

In the space below, note down individual and specific aspects of your professional development and the process of improving yourself as an employee that you need to regularly evaluate (e.g., communication, resume maintenance, networking, etc.). Create and write or draw your own workplace cue for addressing it.

While professional development is challenging and demanding, as you put effort into the various aspects that influence your growth, you will become more and more experienced and prepared for the challenges. Career progression shifts in response to how much effort is put into advancement. Thus, taking time to seek opportunities for professional development will pay off with the impact it will have on your career trajectory.

BACK TO BASICS

B Behavior 1 2 3		Are you actively seeking professional development? How are you balancing your work and personal life?
A Academics 1 2 3		Are you completing your tasks? Do you manage your time? Are you willing to take on new tasks? Is your work meeting your supervisor's expectations?
S Self-care 1 2 3		Are you engaging with your interests? Is your sleep pattern conducive to your work schedule? Are you eating and exercising? Are you managing stress at home and at work? Are you monitoring hygiene?
I Interaction 1 2 3		Are you engaging with your team at work? Are you communicating your work goals to your supervisor?
C Community 1 2 3		Have you identified professional resources? Are you aware of professional opportunities in your community?
S Self-monitoring 1 2 3		Are you keeping track of tasks? Are you aware of your energy levels? Are you realistic about your expectations?

GOALS

Personal:

Aptitude:

Social:

⊕ BACK TO BASICS: RATE YOURSELF

B	**Behavior** 1 2 3	**Comments**
A	**Academics** 1 2 3	**Comments**
S	**Self-care** 1 2 3	**Comments**
I	**Interaction** 1 2 3	**Comments**
C	**Community** 1 2 3	**Comments**
S	**Self-monitoring** 1 2 3	**Comments**

GOALS

Personal:

Aptitude:

Social:

NEXT STEPS

Transitioning into the workplace and adapting to work expectations as a young adult is a considerable challenge. When you add in stressors of interpreting layers of social subtleties and increasing multi-faceted responsibility, young professionals with ASD can struggle even more. Navigating barriers at the workplace will be an ongoing challenge. Having considered the barriers outlined in this text, young adults with ASD can shift to using their strengths to navigate the career web. Once you are aware of the elements of the workplace that cause problems for you, you can address the issues using the strategies given in this text. Be mindful of potential barriers, and be prepared to encounter them with practical skills. Going forward, your next steps will be to continue to gather experience and to increase your aptitude at work in every position you have.

BACK TO BASICS CHART PROFESSIONAL EXAMPLE

B Behavior 1 2 **3**	**Comments** I have been very engaged in looking for new opportunities at work. I have been receptive to feedback and actively practicing new skills.	
A Academics 1 **2** 3	**Comments** I feel competent in my work, but I have a hard time adjusting to new methods and procedures.	
S Self-care 1 **2** 3	**Comments** I am getting enough sleep and taking 5 to 10 minute breaks when needed. I should work harder on making sure I am keeping my workspace uncluttered. I need to stick to my wellness plan.	
I Interaction **1** 2 3	**Comments** I spent a lot of time engaging in small talk with co-workers but sometimes I get distracted. I could do better about collaborating with others when I do not fully understand a task.	
C Community **1** 2 3	**Comments** I have a regular group that I eat lunch with but I have not accepted an invitation to go out with them after work.	
S Self-monitoring 1 **2** 3	**Comments** I am doing a good job at keeping a balance between my personal and professional roles. I could do better about fostering relationships outside of work. I need to do a better job managing my frustrations.	

GUIDED DISCUSSION

In this appendix, discussion points and guiding questions are offered for each chapter by lesson. This information is intended to be a starting point for conversation, and should be built on based on the needs of the group, class, or individual. The suggestions are proposed to provoke thoughts about the material, and we hope that you will build on these suggestions as you choose.

CHAPTER 1: FINDING YOUR PROFESSIONAL NICHE

LESSON 1: NEURODIVERSITY IN THE WORKPLACE

DISCUSSION POINTS

Diversity is a concept that is respected and valued as part of our human experience. Cultural diversity allows us to see the strengths and beauty within each cultural experience. Biodiversity allows us to recognize the genetic variations in species, between species, and within various ecosystems. Neurodiversity allows us to recognize and celebrate the specific differences in the ways people take in, process, and express knowledge. All forms of diversity offer our society as a whole and our work cultures variety and strength, and deserve to be respected.

GUIDING QUESTIONS

- What might you consider your contribution to diversity?

- Describe a time or situation when you were able to focus for long periods of time because something was interesting to you.

- Describe a time that you may have been misunderstood because of your thinking style.

- How do you prefer to take in information?

- How would you describe how you process information?

- How do you prefer to control your expression of information?

- Give an example of how you could advocate for your processing/thinking style.

- What types of expectations do you have for the levels of professional communication?

- What are some potential pitfalls you can plan for?

LESSON 2: FINDING A COMPANY THAT WORKS FOR YOU

DISCUSSION POINTS

The theory of niche construction challenges the long-standing theory of natural selection in which an organism must adjust and adapt to the environment for survival. The same can be true for the construction of a professional niche within a chosen career. Traditional workplaces designed with the expectation that workers will adjust to fit in with expectations is quickly being replaced with more flexible, collaborative work environments. This shift is taking into account the various ways individuals work most effectively, making it a much better landscape for professionals with ASD to advocate for their ideal work environment and to potentially excel in their respective careers.

GUIDING QUESTIONS

- How would you define your potential career?

- How would you describe your professional niche?

- Considering your current job or a previous job, what would be some changes that could be made to be more conducive to your needs?

- What can you identify as your skills and strengths when considering a potential career field?

- Identify some realistic expectations you have about your ideal work environment.

- What factors do you consider when thinking of professional compatibility?

LESSON 3: CREATING YOUR OPTIMAL WORK ENVIRONMENT

DISCUSSION POINTS

To be a responsible and effective employee, as an individual with ASD you must take control of creating your optimal working environment. Rather than expecting your specific skills and strengths to mask your individual needs, identifying your needs, advocating for yourself, and creating your work environment to fit your specific needs is the most effective way of creating a positive work culture. Because you spend so much of your day at work, your environment should be conducive to meeting your particular needs.

- How can you take control of creating your optimal work environment?

- How can you make your environment conducive to meeting your individual needs?

- Describe a situation or example of a positive work culture you have been exposed to in the past.

- How were you able to relate to any of the situations presented in the scenarios?

- How have you advocated for your needs in the past?

LESSON 4: PROFESSIONAL TOOL FOR PROFESSIONAL NICHE DEVELOPMENT

DISCUSSION POINTS

Focusing time and energy early on in your career path on niche development allows you to be better prepared to discuss your passions, strengths, and talents with a potential supervisor. This could allow for a more successful entrance into the world of work. The tool offered in this chapter is an example of professional niche development, which takes into account the talents, skills, interests, and previous work experience to create a solid career choice for individuals with ASD. It is vital to maintain motivation within a career for a person with ASD, so using this tool encourages a person to responsibly combine all three areas to form a balanced professional life.

GUIDING QUESTIONS

- What are your identified strengths, skills, and talents?

- What are your concerns about finding your professional niche?

- How can you make this process seem less overwhelming?

- What stage are you at in your career development?

- Identify some additional strategies that might help you explore your professional niche.

CHAPTER 2: THE INTERVIEW

LESSON 1: PREPARATION FOR INTERVIEW

DISCUSSION POINTS

The process of preparing for an interview with each specific company can be an option for avoiding a potential roadblock in the interview process. By researching the company, the expectations, and leadership of the company, you can identify some areas of common interest, and prepare and rehearse some talking points prior to entering the interview. Another step to take to prepare for an interview is to practice interviewing with someone who can give you honest feedback while also videotaping yourself and providing self-reflective feedback. Spending significant time preparing for an interview can allow an individual with ASD a better opportunity to engage in the process more comfortably and confidently.

GUIDING QUESTIONS

- What makes your resume stand out from others?

- Consider your ideal career. What makes you a qualified candidate for the job?

- What specific topics should you research about a company prior to the interview?

- Who can you identify in your life who would be willing to give you feedback and honestly evaluate your interview skills?

- What is important about a first impression?

- What are some things you need to be mindful of when preparing for an interview?

- Identify some of your qualifications.

- How well do you receive feedback?

- How might doing interview prep work have a positive outcome?

LESSON 2: MAKING THE CONNECTION

DISCUSSION POINTS

The interview is the time when the potential employer is looking for a connection with the interviewee. If there is a potential for a professional relationship or there is some type of connection, that interviewee has a better opportunity for getting an offer. There are many qualified applicants for any given job, but these connections during an interview are what make specific individuals stand out. A personal connection can be made during the introduction phase, the interview process, as well as at the conclusion of the interview.

GUIDING QUESTIONS

- What are some challenges you might face during an interview?

- What skills or trades do you have that could be conversation starter in an interview?

- How do you plan on introducing yourself during an interview?

- How can you recover from a bad first impression?

- How can you plan to make yourself positively stand out in a group interview?

- What are some of your strengths you can identify?

- How can you identify your strengths during an interview?

- If you were to create a personal mission statement for yourself, what would it say about you?

- What are some questions you might ask as you come to the end of the interview?

- How would you define "goodness of fit"?

LESSON 3: FOLLOW UP

Discussion Points

A final way to make connections with the person interviewing you for a job is to follow up with a thank you letter or email. It is important to address the correspondence professionally, thank the interviewer(s), remind them of the position for which you were interviewed, and assure them that you are indeed still interested in the job. Follow up after the interview could also allow you time to clarify questions and further answer any interview questions you feel you did not answer completely. These correspondences should be complete, professional, and brief enough to keep the reader's attention.

Guiding Questions

- What is important to remember about how you should plan to follow up on an interview?

- What are the topics of conversation you should avoid in a follow up to an interview?

- How do you decide what format you should use to follow up various professional situations?

- Describe how you should follow up or react to the interviewer when something doesn't go as planned.

- How would you react to a rejection email?

LESSON 4: PROFESSIONAL TOOL FOR SCRIPTING COMMON INTERVIEW RESPONSES

DISCUSSION POINTS

The majority of interviews include a variation of a common set of questions that each serves a purpose within the interview. An adequate understanding of their purpose can help you develop a good answer while scripting and practice can help you feel more comfortable with the interview process. This increased comfort with the process of the interview can allow for a decrease in the accompanying anxiety regarding the interview stage of the job search. This tool offers individuals sample responses for five of the most asked interview questions, which allows for individuals to script their own responses.

GUIDING QUESTIONS

- Why is it important to practice your responses to potential interview questions?

- How can you make sure your response doesn't seem scripted?

- Besides the top five interview questions provided in the text, what are some additional interview questions you might be asked?

- What limitations should you have when asked the questions "Tell me about yourself?"

CHAPTER 3: DISCLOSURE AND SELF-ADVOCACY

LESSON 1: LEGAL PROTECTION AND ACCOMMODATIONS

DISCUSSION POINTS

Legal protection from discrimination and equal access through reasonable accommodations are available to individuals with disabilities. Workplace discrimination can be an issue for individuals with ASD in the workplace, so developing an understanding of the legal protections offered can be particularly helpful in establishing reasonable accommodations. If discrimination does occur, it is equally important to understand how to navigate the systems in place to report that discrimination and to file a grievance. While it is best to be proactive in the establishment of accommodations, being responsible as a professional includes protecting yourself from mistreatment due to a disability.

GUIDING QUESTIONS

- What types of accommodations do you see yourself needing in the workplace?

- What are some benefits to disclosing your ASD?

- How can you make your disclosure strength-based?

- What are the steps you should take if you are denied an accommodation at work?

- Who should you report your concerns to when you do not feel like your environment is conducive to your ASD?

- Do you see ASD as a barrier to your career goals?

- What are some examples of informal accommodations in the workplace?

- How might the accommodations process as a professional differ from the process you went through as a college student?

- What is meant by the "culture of an accommodation"?

- What are some concerns you have about disclosing?

LESSON 2: ART OF DISCLOSURE

DISCUSSION POINTS

As young professionals consider current employment or future employment possibilities, the various reasons for disclosing should be considered. Once individuals know *why* they are telling others about ASD, they will be more prepared to tackle two other essential considerations for disclosure: *when* and *how*. Knowing how to adapt to the professional context and plan for disclosure in response is an essential part of managing employment for professionals with ASD. This is not an easy task to navigate, but it is one that individuals should be educated about, and for which they should prepare.

GUIDING QUESTIONS

- Describe the impact your disability has on you.

- Why might someone choose not to disclose a disability?

- What implications might disclosure have on you?

- Should there be boundaries to the disclosure process?

- Describe strengths associated with your ASD diagnosis.

LESSON 3: TELL YOUR OWN STORY

DISCUSSION POINTS

When it comes to disclosing something important about yourself to people, it is important to recognize that you cannot control their responses. Unfortunately, many people still have misconceptions about ASD, so if you are considering disclosure, be aware of potential reactions. Sharing information can lead others to have more questions.

GUIDING QUESTIONS

- Do you have a plan to determine a safe person to disclose to if you choose not to disclose to your supervisors?

- Give an example of how you might include a disclosure statement in response to the interview question, "Tell me a little bit about yourself?"

- How have you related to others in the past through a direct tie to ASD?

LESSON 4: PROFESSIONAL TOOL FOR NAVIGATING DISCLOSURE

DISCUSSION POINTS

When young adults with ASD enter the workforce, knowing the right place, the right time, and the right way to disclose can be complicated. While there is no one absolute way to tell others about ASD or to advocate for your accommodation needs as an individual with ASD, having a plan for if, when, how, and to whom you will disclose can ease a lot of stress. Use this tool that outlines the model of disclosure to help you navigate this process as a professional with ASD.

GUIDING QUESTIONS

- Give an example of how you could approach a legal disclosure.

- Give an example of how you define a professional disclosure.

- How are professional and personal disclosures different?

- What is your ideal outcome of disclosing your disability?

CHAPTER 4: PROFESSIONAL WORKPLACE STRUCTURE

LESSON 1: UNDERSTANDING PROFESSIONAL COMMUNICATION

DISCUSSION POINTS

Professional communication involves more than discussing work procedures; it involves communication with peers in addition to reporting directly to a supervisor about work progress. In preparation for the workplace, young adults with ASD will first need to be aware of and able to identify the levels of professional social status of the people with whom they will work. This is important because communication and social engagement expectations will differ depending on professional status. Preparing for this unspoken workplace social order can help you to avoid some common pitfalls due to communication faux pas.

GUIDING QUESTIONS

- What are some of the personal expectations you have for your work?

- How are your strengths a good fit within your workplace?

- What are some ways you actively network?

- How can you make sure that you are respecting the five professional status levels at work?

- Who can you identify to help you navigate company hierarchy, if an issue should arise?

- How can you ensure connections with co-workers?

LESSON 2: COMMUNICATION STRATEGIES

DISCUSSION POINTS

One employment challenge for young professionals, especially those with ASD, is that communication in the workplace has unwritten and unspoken guidelines, which could lead to social confusion and embarrassing miscues. In addition to simple one-on-one verbal conversation, body language, logistical employment components, physical layout of the workplace, and the use of technology-based mobile devices are involved in workplace communication. Verbal speech, body language, and increasingly, tech-based interaction are all co-requisites for mastering professional communication. Practical application of communication strategies occurs through proactive measures and reactive responses. Paying attention to details, being resourceful and creative problem solvers, and adhering to structure when it is established are likely to be strengths of young professionals with ASD. These can be used to navigate the professional communication interactions within and across professional status levels at work.

GUIDING QUESTIONS

- Give an example of an interaction you might have with a supervisor.

- How can you establish your strengths as a professional?

- How are you staying aware of what non-verbal behaviors you display when communicating with others?

- What rules can you establish regarding communication through technology?

- How can you establish that expectations have been properly communicated?

LESSON 3: NAVIGATING PROFESSIONAL MISCUES

DISCUSSION POINTS

Communication difficulties at work due to missing social cues can be embarrassing and, if repeated, could impact sustained employment. While some professional miscues are more consequential than others, not all professional cultures are outright unforgiving of them. Young adults with ASD may misunderstand workplace professional structure and communication cues, and end up in a difficult position socially.

GUIDING QUESTIONS

- How could your literal thinking impact professional communication?

- What are some social miscues that might happen to individuals with ASD?

- How do you resolve social miscues? What are the steps?

- What social miscues have you experienced before?

- What strategies have you used to mitigate the impact of social miscues?

LESSON 4: PROFESSIONAL TOOL FOR MANAGING WORKPLACE COMMUNICATION

DISCUSSION POINTS

An organization chart can help you see the big picture of the professional statuses of your co-workers. It also allows you to consider where you may be positioned on the chart in relation to others. Understanding the professional structure of a workplace can alleviate the pressure of avoiding social miscues at work. Once you are aware of the social interaction norms at work, you will be less likely to misinterpret appropriate behavior and communication. The tool in this chapter should help you to develop an understanding of the hierarchical and social statuses that exist in the workplace.

GUIDING QUESTIONS

- How can you implement strategies from this chapter?

- What impression do you think you leave with others?

- What does it mean to have professional status awareness?

- Where does your envisioned position lie in an organization chart?

CHAPTER 5: STRESS MANAGEMENT

LESSON 1: UNDERSTANDING RESPONSIBILITIES AND IDENTIFYING STRESSORS

DISCUSSION POINTS

The role that stress and anxiety play in the world of young adults with ASD is often overlooked as they navigate the transition to life as new professionals. It is essential that as you begin your journey, that you learn to respect your physical and emotional health. It can be a difficult task to recognize the reaction and impact that stress has on your body, especially for those with ASD. It is your responsibility to recognize the triggers of stress and to learn to mitigate the impact of that resulting stress. Many strategies can be employed to help alleviate the negative implications that stress can have on individuals and on employment.

GUIDING QUESTIONS

- What does stress feel like in your body?

- How is your work performance impacted by stress?

- How does stress impact you physically?

- How can stress impact your emotional responses?

- If changes happen to your schedule, what impact does that have on your level of stress?

- What situations can cause stress for you?

LESSON 2: MANAGING YOUR ENVIRONMENT

DISCUSSION POINTS

A professional work environment can be a place of constant sensory stimulation, which can contribute to stress. Frequent interaction with co-workers, shuffling of papers and tasks, distractions via email or phone calls, the flickering of fluorescent lights, and unique smells and sounds are only a few of the challenges you might face daily on the job. While stress is inevitable in any work situation, it is important for professionals with ASD to recognize when stress is becoming negatively impactful. It is during this time that individuals with ASD can learn to manage their own environment by using their inherent strengths.

GUIDING QUESTIONS

- What coping strategies have worked for you in the past? How might those change for you as a professional?

- What coping strategies listed in this chapter are you willing to explore further?

- What is your established plan to help you manage the stressors as a young professional?

- How might not managing your stress as a young professional have a negative impact on you?

- What things distract you from your task at work?

LESSON 3: RESPONDING TO STRESS IN THE WORKPLACE

DISCUSSION POINTS

Exposure to stress as a new professional is an inevitable part of any job or career path you may take. While some situations or circumstances may provoke more stress than others, the effects of stress do not have to have a long-lasting negative impact on your physical, emotional, or professional well-being. Although young adults with ASD might process through the impact of stress differently, it is possible to manage stressful situations and to mitigate the impact.

GUIDING QUESTIONS

- What are some ways you plan to recharge?

- What are some benefits of personal time?

- You will be responsible for tasks, attending meetings, and sharing space with others at work. It is important to recognize that the choices you make have an impact on those around you and the environment at work. How do you plan to keep your task organized, focused, your space tidy, and your interactions professional?

LESSON 4: PROFESSIONAL TOOL FOR MANAGING STRESS

DISCUSSION POINTS

A wellness plan gives young professionals an opportunity to be proactive in using healthy coping strategies prior to the impact of stress. Staying healthy can help individuals optimize performance, stay alert, and feel good. By being proactive, young professionals can invest energy into managing stress, preventing burnout, and avoiding unhealthy levels of stress, which could have a negative impact. This tool can help promote workplace satisfaction while promoting individual well-being.

GUIDING QUESTIONS

- What types of activities are included in your wellness plan?

- What types of things can distract you from your wellness plan?

- How many hours of sleep do you need to be rested and at your optimal level of function during your working day?

- Who have you identified who could help you make sure you are managing your stress appropriately?

CHAPTER 6: COLLABORATION AND TEAMWORK

LESSON 1: THE PURPOSE OF TEAMWORK

DISCUSSION POINTS

Developing a strong understanding of why teamwork is important can help professionals with ASD embrace this important aspect of a career. Rather than viewing the aspect of collaborating and creating professional work teams as shallow business initiatives that have no true benefit, people with ASD can begin to see the genuine benefit of working on a productive team. Once this purpose is established, workers can spend time developing solid collaborative work skills to make the most of teamwork. Some of the reasons why teamwork is important can be identified as project completion, work sustainability, project completion pace, and contributions of all team members.

GUIDING QUESTIONS

- What do you identify as sources of frustrations in the workplace?

- Why do you think social communication confusion is stressful?

- Identify the purpose or some advantages of teamwork.

- What makes you feel accomplished when you're working in a team?

- How do you plan to stay task-oriented?

- In what ways can competition be good in the workplace? In what ways can competition have a negative impact?

LESSON 2: INDIVIDUAL CONTRIBUTIONS

DISCUSSION POINTS

Every person in a work team has individualized strengths that make them stand out individually, and results in them being hired for their positions. Some people are very good at networking and connecting people and ideas, while others are very good at analyzing and categorizing information into a logical order. Some team members are very technologically sound while others are better at interpersonal interactions. Regardless of the strengths and skills a person brings to the team, they should be recognized and honored. Professionally, people with ASD tend to have significant strengths that can be true assets for any business.

GUIDING QUESTIONS

- In what ways do you value the relationship with others on your team?

- What talents and skills do you bring to group work?

- How do you plan to monitor your expectations and reactions to others on your team?

- What do you identify as your work-related strengths?

- How can you acknowledge the strengths of others?

- What roles have you taken in a group project?

LESSON 3: CONFLICT RESOLUTION

DISCUSSION POINTS

Collaborative teamwork can also contribute to workplace conflict. Successful teams focus not only on the completion of a project, but also on recognizing team members' strengths, communicating effectively, negotiating so everyone feels valued, and reaching the goal together. With so many opportunities for social miscues, conflict is a real possibility, but the fear of that conflict should not be a reason to avoid working collaboratively. Employing responsible conflict resolution strategies can be effective in the health and sustainability of work teams.

GUIDING QUESTIONS

- In what ways do you worry about conflict within a team?

- What strategies do you have to help you resolve conflict if it happens?

- What types of signals can you look for to understand your role on a team?

- How might an unbalanced team impact success?

LESSON 4: PROFESSIONAL TOOL FOR DEFINING YOUR ROLE IN A TEAM

DISCUSSION POINTS

A component to being successful in the work setting involves being able to use your skills and knowledge in the way you prefer, that not only allows you to be successful in your career, but also to be comfortable and happy in doing so. These preferences can help you outline your roles in any collaborative team along with the harmonizing roles you need to identify in your co-workers. Although working on a team requires an incredible amount of cognitive and social energy, this tool can allow you to identify your strengths and the strengths of others to develop the most effective work team.

GUIDING QUESTIONS

- What can you identify as different styles of work?
- How can you value other members of your team?
- Discuss the role of your primary preference.
- Discuss the harmonizing role in your work team.
- How might a collaborator and thinker pair within a team?

CHAPTER 7: WATER COOLER CULTURE

LESSON 1: THE HIDDEN RULES

DISCUSSION POINTS

These informal and unspoken rules are some of the obstacles that could interfere with sustained employment for professionals with ASD. The primary objective for workers with ASD is to focus on the main duties of the job and completing the work to a high level of success. These informal practices could take away from the focus on work, and encourage individuals to focus more energy on navigating another set of social rules. This could, in return, diminish the work output of those professionals. However, the rules around these informal exchanges in the workplace are vital to understand. The first step in developing tools to navigate the work environment is to understand what these unwritten social rules of the work environment are, and what purpose they serve.

GUIDING QUESTIONS

- What are some examples of company culture?
- What are some informal rules that you can identify about your place of work?
- Identify some topics that are appropriate for small talk.
- What are some strategies that you can identify to help you practice small talk and sharing the conversation?
- How can you initiate a small talk conversation at work?
- Why is it important to have peer-to-peer interactions at work?
- Discuss the differences in professional communication methods.
- What can you identify as some examples of professional social nuances?

- What are some differences between professional and personal communication?

- Identify some environmental sensitivities you might experience, and how that might impact your small talk with co-workers.

LESSON 2: LEARNING THROUGH CASUAL INTERACTIONS

DISCUSSION POINTS

Informal office gatherings can include holiday parties hosted by the company, lunch gatherings, Friday afternoon drinks, or occasional shared lunch times. While these are often optional and do not directly affect the job as defined, they do serve a purpose. These times together are when colleagues develop trusting relationships with each other that help build morale on the job. The social nature of these gatherings can be overwhelming to people with ASD, so many opt out of participating. Opting out of all of these experiences, however, may place those with ASD on the outside of the work circle. By not taking advantage of these opportunities to make connections, co-workers may feel that they are not engaged members of the work team.

GUIDING QUESTIONS

- How does team morale impact performance?

- What impact can your attendance at informal gatherings have on your collaboration with co-workers?

- What are some appropriate reasons to opt out of informal social gatherings at work?

- How can you plan to recharge after a work social event?

- What are some unspoken social rules of work that you can identify?

LESSON 3: JOINING IN THE CULTURE

DISCUSSION POINTS

Difficulties associated with ASD lie with developing meaning from context and understanding social cues; these ever-changing social rules create immense confusion in the work setting. They are not only informal and unspoken, but the expectations shift from situation to situation and from person to person, also making them inconsistent and unpredictable.

GUIDING QUESTIONS

- How can you plan to navigate the "water cooler culture" of your workplace?

- How can you take ownership of your professional growth?

- What are some misunderstood social rules that might be common for individuals with ASD?

- How can you plan to monitor you interactions with others?

LESSON 4: PROFESSIONAL TOOL FOR CREATING SOCIAL RULES

DISCUSSION POINTS

Due to the unpredictability and inconsistent nature of the rules associated with this water cooler culture in the workplace, it is imperative that individuals with ASD develop strategies to help navigate this confusing aspect of employment. While there is no evidence-based approach to navigating these unspoken social rules that neurotypical workers understand intuitively, professionals with ASD can develop a rulebook to help them overcome this confusion. While it may continue to be difficult to generalize the rules to other interactions, this tool may offer some degree of understanding to help mute some of the social confusion and lessen the potential for professional isolation or loss of employment due to breaking these social rules.

GUIDING QUESTIONS

- Who have you identified as someone to give you feedback about your interactions with others at work?

- What types of rules should you include in your rulebook?

- What professional rules have you already developed?

- Why is it important to understand the purpose of any rule?

- How can a rulebook help you navigate the social world of work?

CHAPTER 8: PROFESSIONAL GROWTH

LESSON 1: STARTING OVER IS OKAY

DISCUSSION POINTS

Individuals with ASD in the workplace will benefit from regular professional development. Practicing and learning more about the field in order to progress through it is a linear and logical concept. Through this process it is possible that a professional may come to the realization that the current place of employment or current field is not the right fit. As previously discussed in this text, finding goodness of fit is vital to maintain employability. Sometimes this means starting over in a different company or a different field. Starting over is a positive option when handled responsibly and with caution.

GUIDING QUESTIONS

- What are some ways you can assess whether you are in the wrong career or career field?

- How might starting over help you in your long-term career goals?

- What are some of the potential barriers involved in professional development?

- What skills and strategies did you learn transitioning into college that you could apply to your transition to the workplace?

- What is a sign that your personal wellness is taking a toll as a result of work stress?

LESSON 2: ONGOING PROFESSIONAL DEVELOPMENT

DISCUSSION POINTS

As a young professional, you will develop into a more marketable job applicant and a more prepared and skilled employee by intentionally seeking career-advancing opportunities and staying aware of progression in your field. This requires diligent work, and typically occurs in coordination with or in addition to an employment position. Professional development is an active and intentional investment in your future career.

GUIDING QUESTIONS

- What is the purpose of professional development?

- What are the five professional development components outlined in this chapter?

- How are you seeking opportunities for growth in each of these five professional growth areas?

- Why does your personal appearance matter when it comes to professional development opportunities?

- How can your special interests improve your professional development work?

LESSON 3: EVALUATION AND FEEDBACK

DISCUSSION POINTS

Evaluations of your performance and fit will occur as early as the interview phase. Part of your supervisor's responsibility will be to ensure you are trained and prepared for your own duties. Evaluations at work may be formal and routine or they may be more informal and infrequent. While individuals with ASD may prefer direct feedback, your supervisor may be less clear when offering feedback. If this is the case, and your supervisor's vague feedback is making it difficult for you to assess your performance, ask for clarification. Once your preference for direct feedback is known, it may take some of the pressure off of the person giving you feedback.

GUIDING QUESTIONS:

- At what point do others begin to evaluate you in the job search process?

- How do regular evaluations influence your work progress?

- What is the difference between formal and informal evaluations? Give an example of each type.

- How do you prefer to receive feedback?

- How can you convey your preference for feedback in a discussion with your supervisor?

LESSON 4: PROFESSIONAL TOOLS FOR PROFESSIONAL DEVELOPMENT

DISCUSSION POINTS

Professional development requires young professionals to monitor their production during work times and their adherence to self-care measures to maintain employment. There are constantly new forms of input in the workplace that individuals with ASD have difficulty filtering. Simple self-evaluation tools, such as the pneumonic devices outlined in this lesson, can prompt young professionals with ASD to consider their progress in their current position and to direct their preparedness measures for futures positions. This tool and others like it can help professionals with ASD remind themselves of the necessary steps to monitor the important aspects of employment.

GUIDING QUESTIONS

- Why is it important to seek professional development?

- What are some easy ways to prompt yourself to take action?

- Who can you identify at work to help support you as you seek professional development opportunities?

- How can you make sure your prompts and cues for professional development are practical at work?

RESUME TOOLS

Use the example resume and resume template to draft your own resume.

Erin Maynard

1234 West Fairview Drive • Norris, TN, 37890
Home: (615)123-4567
Cell: (615)123-6789
Erin.Maynard@example.com

EDUCATION

University of Tennessee at Chattanooga   **2012–Present**
Bachelor of Science in Psychology   **(Projected Graduation: May 2016)**

EXPERIENCE

MoSAIC Program—Disability Resource Center—U.T. Chattanooga   **2014–Present**
Research Assistant

- Organize progress reports for students in the Mosaic program
- Assist in the development of a resource data base specific to research of Autism Spectrum Disorder
- Maintain confidentiality

W Squared   **June–August 2014**
Information Technology Summer Intern

- Configured computers
    » Installed software (e.g. Microsoft Word, Adobe Flash, Adobe Reader, Adobe Acrobat)
    » Added computers to local domain
    » Backed-up computers to an external drive and transfered information to a new computer
- Assisted in customer services
- Compiled hardware and software inventory

First United Methodist Church Day Camp   **2007–2013**
Camp Counselor for K–4th Grade

- Set up activities
- Organized talent shows
- Supervised children

ACHIEVEMENTS

- Student Representative on Disability Resource Center Advisory Board   2013–Present
- Speaker at 2nd Annual DiversAbility Event at UTC   2014
- Alternate Spring Break participant at UTC   2013
- First United Methodist Church Youth Council   2010–2012
- Model United Nations Conference   2009, 2011

VOLUNTEER EXPEREINCE

- Joe's Storehouse Food Pantry
- Open Table Soup Kitchen
- TEAMeffort Service Organization
- Chattanooga Autism Center
- Chattanooga Autism Awareness Walk

COMPUTER SKILLS

- Proficient with Microsoft Word, Excel, PowerPoint, Access, Internet, Data Collection, and Research

*References Available Upon Request

Figure C.1 Example of a resume

RESUME TEMPLATE

Name: _____

Address: _____
_____
Number: _____
Email: _____

EDUCATION

University: _____

Degree: _____

Expected graduation date: _____

University GPA: _____

WORK EXPERIENCE

Company: _____   **Start/End Date of Employment:** _____

Position Title: _____

- Duties: _____
- Duties: _____
- Duties: _____
- Duties: _____

Company: _____   **Start/End Date of Employment:** _____

Position Title: _____

- Duties: _____
- Duties: _____
- Duties: _____
- Duties: _____

Company: _____   **Start/End Date of Employment:** _____

Position Title: _____

- Duties: _____
- Duties: _____
- Duties: _____
- Duties: _____

SKILLS AND CERTIFICATIONS

_____
_____
_____

ACTIVITIES AND HONORS

_____
_____
_____

REFERENCES

Name: _____   **Contact Number:** _____

Position: _____

Name: _____   **Contact Number:** _____

Position: _____

SAMPLE INTERVIEW QUESTIONS

1. How did you hear about this position?

2. Tell me about an accomplishment you are most proud of.

3. What diversity can you bring into this position?

4. Give a time when you went above and beyond the requirements for a project.

5. What are your strengths?

6. What are your weaknesses?

7. What is one thing that you are passionate about? (Limit this to two to three minutes.)

8. Who would you consider the most influential person in your life?

9. How do you keep yourself on task?

10. How would those closest to you describe you?

11. Where do you see yourself in five years? Ten years?

12. What are some things you learned about yourself in the past five years?

13. Why was there a gap in your employment?

14. What can you offer us that someone else can't?

15. Are you willing to relocate?

16. Are you willing to travel?

17. Tell me about a time you made a mistake and how you handled it.

18. What is your dream job?

19. What does an ideal working week look like?

20. What are some areas of growth you would like to improve on?

21. How do you plan to continue growing your work skills?

22. Give three words that describe you.

23. Tell me how you handled a difficult situation.

24. What are some ways you manage stress?

25. Why should we hire you?

26. Are you willing to work holidays/weekends?

27. What motivates you?

28. What's your availability for work?

29. Tell me about a time when you disagreed with your supervisor. How did you come to a mutual understanding?

30. How do you handle pressure?

31. What are your career goals, and how do you plan on bringing those skills to this job?

32. Are you a leader or a follower?

33. If you have an issue with a co-worker, what steps would you take to resolve it?

34. What are some things you like to do in your free time?

35. How would your personality contribute to the workplace atmosphere?

36. How do you define success?

37. What makes you uncomfortable?

38. What are some of your leadership experiences?

39. What questions haven't I asked you?

40. What questions do you have for me?

REFERENCES

Atwood, T. (1999) The discovery of "Aspie" criteria. Available at www.tonyattwood.com.au/index. php/component/content/article?id=79:the-discovery-of-aspie-criteria, accessed on December 11, 2015.

American Psychological Association (2014) Coping with stress at work. Available at www.apa.org/ helpcenter/work-stress.aspx, accessed on January 29, 2016.

Bissonnette, B. (2013) *Asperger's Syndrome Workplace Survival Guide: A Neurotypical's Secrets for Success.* Philadelphia, PA: Jessica Kingsley Publishers.

Briel, L. W. and Getzel, E. E. (2014) In their own words: The career planning experiences of college students with ASD. *Journal of Vocational Rehabilitation 40*, 195–202.

CDC (Center for Disease Control) (2014) CDC estimates 1 in 68 children has been identified with autism spectrum disorder. Press release. Available at www.cdc.gov/media/releases/2014/p0327-autism-spectrum-disorder.html, accessed on November 22, 2015.

Crum, A. J., Salovey, P. and Achor, S. (2013) Rethinking stress: The role of mindsets in determining the stress response. *Journal of Personality and Social Psychology 104*, 4, 716–733.

Erbentraut, J. (2015) How these 4 major companies are tackling the autism unemployment rate. Available at www.huffingtonpost.com, accessed on November 6, 2015.

Fast, Y. (2004) *Employment for Individuals with Asperger Syndrome or Non-Verbal Learning Disability: Stories and Strategies.* London: Jessica Kingsley Publishers.

Grandin, T. (2011) *The Way I See It: A personal Look at Autism and Asperger's.* Arlington, TX: Future Horizons, Inc.

Grapel, J. N., Cicchetti, D. V. and Volkmar, F. R. (2015) Sensory features as diagnostic criteria for autism: Sensory features in autism. *Yale Journal of Biology and Medicine 88*, 1, 69–71, March 4.

Green, A. (2015) The 10 most common interview questions. Available at http://money.usnews.com/ money/careers/slideshows/the-10-most-common-interview-questions/9, accessed on November 25, 2015.

Griswold, A. (2014) Companies are hiring autistic workers to boost the bottom line. Available at www. slate.com, accessed on November 6, 2015.

Hendrickx, S. (2009) *Asperger Syndrome and Employment.* London: Jessica Kingsley Publishers.

Holwerda, A., van der Klink, J. J., Groothoff, J. W. and Brouwer, S. (2012) Predictors for work participation in individuals with autism spectrum disorder: A systematic review. *Journal of Occupational Rehabilitation 22*, 3, 333–352.

Hurlbutt, K. and Chalmers, L. (2004) Employment and adults with Asperger Syndrome. *Focus on Autism and Other Developmental Disabilities 19*, 4, 215–222.

Kopelson, K. (2015) "Know thy work and do it": The rhetorical-pedagogical work of employment and workplace guides for adults with "high-functioning" autism. *College English 77*, 6, July.

Management Study Guide (2015) Importance of team and team work. Available at www. managementstudyguide.com/importance-of-team.htm, accessed on December 10, 2015.

Meeks, L., Masterson, T., Rigler, M. and Quinn, E. (2016) *Parties, Dorms and Social Norms: A Crash Course in Safe Living for Young Adults on the Autism Spectrum.* London: Jessica Kingsley Publishers.

Meeks, L. M., Masterson, T. L. and Westlake, G. (2015) Career Connect: A collaborative employment resource model for university students with ASD. *Career Planning & Adult Development Journal 31*, 4.

Meyer, R. N. (2001) *Asperger Syndrome Employment Workbook: An Employment Workbook for Adults with Asperger Syndrome.* London: Jessica Kingsley Publishers.

Murza, K. A. and Nye, C. (2013) Pragmatic language intervention for adults with Asperger Syndrome or high-functioning autism: A feasibility study. *Contemporary Issues in Communication Science and Disorders 40*, 85–97.

National Autistic Society (2012) Untapped talent: A guide to employing people with autism. Available at www.adultasd.org/untapped-talent-a-guide-to-employing-people-with-autism, accessed May 2016.

National Sleep Foundation (2016) How much sleep do we really need? Available at https:// sleepfoundation.org/how-sleep-works/how-much-sleep-do-we-really-need, accessed May 2016.

Ozonoff, S., Dawson, G. and McPartland, J. C. (2015) *A Parent's Guide to High-Functioning Autism Spectrum Disorder: How to Meet the Challenges and Help Your Child to Thrive.* Second Edition. New York: Guilford Press.

Post, M., Haymes, L., Storey, K., Loughrey, T. and Campbell, C. (2014) Understanding stalking behaviors by individuals with Autism Spectrum Disorders and recommended prevention strategies for school settings. *Journal of Autism and Developmental Disorders 44*, 11, 2698–2706.

Richards, J. (2015) Asperger syndrome and employment inclusion: Towards practices informed by theories of contemporary employment. *IPED: Interdisciplinary perspectives on equality and diversity 1*, 1, 1–17.

Rigler, M., Rutherford, A., and Quinn, E. (2015a) I*ndependence, Social, and Study Strategies for Young Adults with Autism Spectrum Disorder: The BASICS College Curriculum.* Philadelphia, PA: Jessica Kingsley Publishers.

Rigler, M., Rutherford, A. and Quinn, E. (2015b) *Developing Identity, Strengths, and Self-Perception for Young Adults with Autism Spectrum Disorder: The BASICS College Curriculum.* Philadelphia, PA: Jessica Kingsley Publishers.

Rigler, M., Rutherford, A. and Quinn, E. (2015c) *Turning Skills and Strengths into Careers for Young Adults with Autism Spectrum Disorder. The BASICS College Curriculum,* Philadelphia, PA: Jessica Kingsley Publishers.

Schall, C., Wehman, P. and McDonough, J. L. (2012) Transition from school to work for students with autism spectrum disorders: Understanding the process and achieving better outcomes. *Pediatric Clinics of North America 59*, 1, 189–202.

Scott, M., Falkmer, M., Girdler, S. and Falkmer, T. (2015) Viewpoints on factors for successful employment for adults with Autism Spectrum Disorder. *PLoS ONE 10*, 10.

Scott-Phillips, T., Laland, K. N., Shucker, D. M., Dickins, T. E. and West, S. S. (2013) The niche construction perspective: A critical appraisal. *Evolution 68*, 5 1231–1243.

Simone, R. (2010) *Asperger's on the Job: Must Have Advice for People with Asperger's or High Functioning Autism and the Employers, Educators, and Advocates.* Arlington, TX: Future Horizons, Inc.

Silberman, S. (2015) *NeuroTribes: The Legacy of Autism and the Future of Neurodiversity.* New York: Avery.

Stewart, J. B. (2013) Looking for a lesson in Google perks. *The New York Times*, March 15.

Tantam, D. and van Deurzen, E. (2014) *Emotional Well-being and Mental Health: A Guide for Counsellors & Psychotherapists.* Sage Publications.

van Lange, P.A.M. (2015) Generalized trust: Lessons from genetics and culture. *Current Directions in Psychological Science 24*, 71–76.

Wilkie, C. (2013) *Young adults with autism seek out white-collar careers for the first time.* Available at www. huffingtonpost.com, accessed on November 6, 2015.

INDEX